Pub 956

*Twayne's English Authors Series*

EDITOR OF THIS VOLUME

Sarah Smith

*Tufts University*

# *James Hogg*

TEAS 311

# James Hogg

*"The Ettrick Shepherd" by William Nicholson reproduced courtesy of Mrs. C. M. White*

# JAMES HOGG

By NELSON C. SMITH
*University of Victoria*

TWAYNE PUBLISHERS
A DIVISION OF G. K. HALL & CO., BOSTON

821.7
H716 S
1980

**Library of Congress Cataloging in Publication Data**

Smith, Nelson C.
James Hogg.

(Twayne's English authors series; TEAS 311)
Bibliography: p. 181-83
Includes index.
1.   Hogg, James, 1770-1835
— Criticism and interpretation.
PR4792.S53        821'.7        80-16813
ISBN 0-8057-6803-3

To KAREN,

IAN, and ALISON

# Contents

# About the Author

Associate Professor of English at the University of Victoria, Nelson C. Smith was born in New York City in 1940. He grew up in the Detroit area, and received his education from Princeton (A.B.), Oberlin (M.A.T.), and the University of Washington (Ph.D.). He moved to British Columbia in 1967 and became a Canadian citizen in 1973; his teaching fields include British, American, and Canadian fiction and the theory of the novel. He lives and makes wine in Victoria with his singer-wife, Karen, and their two children.

Prof. Smith has written a study of the Gothic novelist Ann Radcliffe, *The Art of Gothic* (New York: Arno Press, 1980), and was co-author with Peter Evans and others of *Language: B.C.* (Victoria: Ministry of Education, 1976), a provincial study of English and language arts teaching in elementary and secondary schools. He has contributed articles and reviews to *Melville Society Extracts*, *Studies in English Literature*, and *College Composition and Communication*. He is currently working on early Canadian fiction and computer-assisted learning projects for remedial composition.

# Preface

The last century has not been kind to the reputation of James Hogg, the Ettrick Shepherd. First recognized as one of Scotland's important poets, second only to Robert Burns in his lyrics, Hogg later became known as a superb writer of supernatural stories and was avidly sought after to contribute to the popular literary annuals. On his first trip to London, at the age of sixty-one, he was feted and honored as the most remarkable of Scottish writers; yet after his death three years later in 1835 his reputation waned, becoming confined to the region of his birth. For most of the rest of the nineteenth century, he was remembered as a song writer, a voice of the shepherds who still sang his lyrics, such as "When the Kye comes Hame," "A Boy's Song," "Donald M'Donald," and "Charlie is my Darling," or who knew his most famous short narratives, "Kilmeny" and "The Witch of Fife." Queen Victoria noted in her diary of August 15, 1871, that she sat in the garden of Holyrood, reading "out of a volume of poems by the Ettrick Shepherd, full of beautiful things."[1] Little notice was taken of the prose fiction, although some editions of tales continued to appear.

By the early twentieth century, Hogg's name and works had become more obscure. His eldest daughter published a biography and a selection of poems in the 1880s, and four brief biographies which appeared before 1940 attempted to set straight the details of Hogg's life, but failed to excite much interest in his works. Finally, in 1947 a new edition of a work little known or little regarded in Hogg's lifetime, *The Confessions and Memoirs of a Justified Sinner*, appeared with an introduction by André Gide and was recognized as a minor masterpiece. Now James Hogg the poet was all but forgotten. More recently, however, thanks to increased Scottish nationalism, scholarly editions of some of the Shepherd's works have appeared, including his second important novel, his autobiographical pieces, his best historical tale, and some selected poems. Still, however, much of Hogg's work is available only in reprints of the 1865 collection or in original editions and periodicals, while critical attention has been minimal.

Thus the reaction to Hogg's works has been a function of changing emphases as well as the erratic availability of the writings themselves. Moreover, the collected edition is itself erratic: it includes, for example, only about 60 percent of the fiction, with some of that in abridged form, and a greater part, though by no means all, of the poetry. Also, the selection is uneven, even given that Hogg was an uneven writer. Many of the stories included in *The Works of the Ettrick Shepherd* are far from Hogg's best, being repetitive and of little significance, whereas some of his best pieces have never been reprinted; the *Confessions* and the *Three Perils of Man* exist in abridged forms which lack power and humor, and a third novel, *The Three Perils of Woman*, which contains one of his best female characters, does not appear at all. Obviously some kind of evaluation of Hogg's achievement is needed, one based on *all* his works and on their interrelationship. The latter is crucial, since Hogg did not really develop as a writer. His later poems and stories show little significant advance either in theme or technique over the earlier ones; the prose, which largely superseded the poetry in his later life, does not differ materially from that poetry. His best works span the genres, for his successes occur in novel, short story, sketch, lyric, narrative poem, parody, and autobiography.

This study is such an overall evaluation. It attempts to bring together Hogg's diverse accomplishments and to come to some kind of judgment as to his strengths and weaknesses. Some time must first be spent on his life and on his nonfiction work, since most of his later works derive from his peasant beginnings and his involvement in the literary life of Edinburgh, including his important friendship with and devotion to Sir Walter Scott. The next chapter deals in general terms with the imaginative literature, showing Hogg's typical approaches and techniques in his conventional poetry and fiction and indicating his common themes, clear strengths, and obvious flaws. Three chapters then focus on his major accomplishments in the areas of historical, comic, and supernatural works, the areas for which he deserves most attention today; in these chapters will be found more extensive discussions of his major writings, including both those recognized in the past and others which have undeservedly received no consideration whatsoever. The result will reveal an author who,

*Preface*

though clearly not among the first rank of literary artists, has written more and better work than he has generally been given credit for. After all these years, a reputation should be just.

The author wishes to express his appreciation to the Canada Council and to the University of Victoria for supporting a sabbatical leave in Great Britain so that he could find and read the uncollected works and rare editions, manuscripts, and letters of Hogg, most of them in the National Library of Scotland; to Douglas S. Mack, for taking time to answer questions; and to William F. Irmscher, for his constant generosity. In addition, the aid of Dawn Hood and Karen Smith in preparing the manuscript has been invaluable. Any flaws that may remain, however, are naturally the author's responsibility.

NELSON C. SMITH

*University of Victoria, British Columbia*

# Chronology

1770   James Hogg born, probably late November, at Ettrickhall Farm, Selkirkshire, the second son of a tenant farmer.

1777   Leaves school after a few months following father's failure.

1777-  Serves as menial laborer for several masters.
1787

1788   Becomes shepherd for Mr. Laidlaw of Willenslee; encouraged to read and to reteach himself writing.

1790-  Works as shepherd for Mr. Laidlaw of Blackhouse in
1800   Yarrow; begins to write verse and contributes poem to *Scots Magazine* in 1794.

1800   "Donald M'Donald" becomes popular throughout Scotland.

1801   *Scottish Pastorals.*

1802   Meets Walter Scott.

1807   *The Mountain Bard* and *The Shepherd's Guide.*

1810   Failing to maintain farm or to procure shepherd's work, moves to Edinburgh to become a writer; *The Forest Minstrel*; edits and writes most of *The Spy*, a weekly periodical which lasts a year.

1813   *The Queen's Wake* makes his reputation.

1815   Receives gift of farm at Altrive Lake from Duke of Buccleuch; *The Pilgrims of the Sun.*

1816   *Mador of the Moor*; *The Poetic Mirror.*

1817   *Blackwood's Magazine* founded, to which Hogg contributes regularly; *Dramatic Tales.*

1818   *The Brownie of Bodsbeck.*

1819   *Jacobite Relics, First Series.*

1820   *Winter Evening Tales*; marries Margaret Phillips.

1821   Leases Mount Benger Farm, leading to financial difficulties for next nine years; *Jacobite Relics, Second Series.*

1822   *Poetical Works*; *The Three Perils of Man*; Christopher North's "Noctes Ambrosianae" in *Blackwood's* begins.

1823   *The Three Perils of Woman.*

1824 *The Private Memoirs and Confessions of a Justified Sinner.*
1825 *Queen Hynde.*
1829 *The Shepherd's Calendar.*
1831 *Songs.*
1832 Visits London to arrange for a collected edition of his fiction, but publisher goes bankrupt after first volume of *Altrive Tales* appears; Scott dies; *A Queer Book.*
1834 *Familiar Anecdotes of Sir Walter Scott; Lay Sermons.*
1835 *Tales of the Wars of Montrose*; dies November 21.

# CHAPTER 1

# *The Making of a Writer*

T HE Ettrick Shepherd was probably the best known of all his Scottish contemporaries save Scott. Not only did he write his autobiography three times over the course of the last thirty years of his life, but his stories and poems appeared regularly, signed from his farms at Altrive Lake and Mount Benger, in the leading literary magazines of Edinburgh. In addition, he wrote letters to journals, contributed to annuals, and received visitors of all ranks at his farm, much to the depletion of his resources, financial and creative. Moreover, Hogg was a public figure in quite another way, one which would influence much of his writing, for in 1822 John Wilson ("Christopher North") began the popular and long-running series of table-talk sketches called "Noctes Ambrosianae," in which a group of characters representing the *Blackwood's* writers conversed on topics ranging from public morals to science and literature. The most impressive character in this series was the "Ettrick Shepherd," an unsophisticated, part-buffoon, part-rustic philosopher, who drank heavily and professed at various times both incredible ignorance and marvellous sagacity. Nineteenth-century critics compared the character with Falstaff and Socrates, and, though by no means the real James Hogg, it was an image accepted by many people, including Hogg himself when the portrait was flattering.

What Wilson had done, however, was to exaggerate many of Hogg's characteristics—his simplicity; his love of sport, eating, and drinking; his ambition and desire for acceptance—and to capitalize on the most remarkable fact of his career: that he had only a few months of schooling, at the age of six, and that he had to relearn reading and writing by himself when he was almost twenty. For the name by which he was known reflects the literal truth: until his fortieth year, Hogg worked as a cowherd, man-of-

15

all-work, tenant farmer, and shepherd among the hills and valleys of Selkirkshire. This background, obviously, colors all his work: his literary training, his styles, his techniques, and usually his successes come from the ballads, folk-tales, and religion of the Border peasantry, almost uncontaminated by contact with the traditions of English literature. Later, when he determined to go to Edinburgh and embark upon a career as writer—itself an amazing project considering his background and age—he would take his models from his contemporaries, notably Scott and Burns. His simple, unintellectual, generous character, coupled with his professed literary ambition and desire for acceptance, marks everything that he said and wrote. Had he written just competently, he would have been noteworthy. As it is, he can be admired for considerable achievements regardless of his background. Scott wrote to Lord Byron of Hogg: "He is a wonderful creature for his opportunities, which were far inferior to those of the generality of Scottish peasants. Burns, for instance, . . . had an education not much worse than the sons of many gentlemen in Scotland. But poor Hogg literally could neither read nor write till a very late period of his life; and when he first distinguished himself by his poetical talent, could neither spell nor write grammar."[1] The nineteenth-century contention that Hogg represents, after Burns, "the greatest poet that has sprung from the bosom of the common people" of Scotland[2] still remains a fair judgment.

## I  *Shepherd of the Ettrick*

James Hogg was born in the small cottage of Ettrickhall Farm toward the end of November 1770. The exact date is unknown, and Hogg himself always misdated it January 25, 1772, for reasons that have caused much speculation. His daughter, Mrs. Garden, suggests that the misdating resulted from his poor memory as well as the careless keeping of records; she assigns November 25 as his probable birthdate. Hogg writes, in "Storms," that years were generally reckoned not by dates but by memorable events, so that an error of one year—the winter of 1770-71 or 1771-72—seems insignificant. His critics, though, even in his lifetime mocked the "coincidence" of the January birthdate being the same as that of Robert Burns, and at their most uncharitable suggested that Hogg was creating a parallel in order to further the acceptance of his early works. In any event, Hogg was shown, late in his life, the parish register of Ettrick which listed his baptism on December 9, 1770. Probably the Burns parallel *was* in his mind early in his career, but he continued the "deception" comically as a kind of private joke. In 1834 he told a memorial dinner in Peebles how he was born on the same day as Burns amid similar terrible snowstorms, and in a letter later that year remarked facetiously, "What would I give to have a son on the 25th of January, for I am sure he would turn out the greatest poet of us all."[3]

If the exact date is not terribly significant, however, his parents and his place of birth remain crucial. At his second son's birth, Robert Hogg was economically and socially successful, having the control of two farms, Ettrickhall and Ettrickhouse, and having reached a position of some standing in the small parish after beginning life as a shepherd. It was still a humble enough position —and one that would shortly collapse in bankruptcy—although he could claim descent from William Hogg, the "wild boar," and several other "hardy Hoggs of Fauldshope," yeomen and retainers praised in an old ballad "For courage, blood, an' bane;/For the Wild Boar of Fauldshope,/Like him was never nane." The Hoggs were also known for witchcraft, since among them was "the famous witch of Fauldshope, who so terribly hectored Mr. Michael Scott [the famous medieval warlock] by turning him into a hare, and hunting him with his own dogs."[4]

Hogg's mother, born Margaret Laidlaw, also came from ancient stock. The Laidlaws, according to Mrs. Garden, "were well known in the district as shrewd, clever people,"[5] and Hogg would work for several of his distant relatives who had successfully maintained their farms while the Hoggs had failed to do so. The most fascinating character in her immediate family was her father, the renowned William Laidlaw of Craik, or Will o' Phaup, whose chief claims to local fame were his capacity for brandy, his speed in foot-racing, his ability in fighting, and, primarily, his being "the last man of this wild region, who heard, saw, and conversed with the fairies; and that not once or twice, but at sundry times and seasons."[6] Some of the occasions, detailed in Hogg's sketch of his grandfather, might have been optical illusions, but Hogg writes, "though Will was a man whose character had a deep tinge of the superstitions of his own country, he was besides a man of probity, truth, and honour, and never told that for the truth which he did not believe to be so" (*Tales*, 410).

Not only did Hogg grow up sharing these superstitions and hearing the stories of his ancestors, he also received from his mother the chief, almost the sole literary influence of his life: the whole Scottish oral tradition passed on from the earliest minstrels. Margaret Hogg, according to the editor of the *Works*, was "remarkable for her Border lore, in the shape of ballads, songs, and traditional stories, so that . . . her cottage was a favourite resort of the shepherds of Ettrick and Yarrow" (*Poems*, x). Hogg's elder brother notes that James "was remarkably fond of hearing stories, and our mother to keep us boys quiet would often tell us tales of kings, giants, knights, fairies, kelpies, brownies, etc., etc. These stories fixed both our eyes and attention, and our mother got forward with her housewifery affairs in a more regular way. She also often repeated to us the metre psalms, and accustomed us to repeat them after her. . . . After [James] read with fluency, the historical part of the Bible was his chief delight, and no person whom I have been acquainted with knew it so well."[7] Nearly all the Shepherd's best work derives directly from the ballad and oral traditions imparted by his mother. Moreover, her fame as a teller of the old tales and songs led to her son's meeting with Walter Scott, who would become Hogg's adviser, friend, and, in a feudal sense, liege-lord.

Ettrick parish, about forty miles south of Edinburgh, was small, isolated, and devoted almost entirely to the raising of sheep; the entire county of Selkirk had once been Ettrick Forest, a royal hunting preserve, and there were other historic associations with Sir William Wallace, Border feuds, and the persecutions of the Covenanters. By Hogg's time, Ettrick was a forest in name only, as indicated by a letter from the novelist John Galt, suggesting that Hogg transplant some of his fairies and hobgoblins to Canadian forests: "To be sure, there is some difficulty in the inhabitant of a treeless forest conceiving a forest of trees, [but I would advise you] to collect all the mops, besoms, brushes and kirn staffs, and stick them in your midden, in an inverted position, and then sit down and draw from the models, supplying from your poetical lumber-room bark branches and leaves, taking care not to show on the trunks anything like a twig, till you have made them each and all severally as high as the Melville monument."[8]

In 1792 the *Statistical Account of Scotland* reported of Ettrick: "This parish possesses no advantage. The nearest market town is 15 miles distant. The roads to all of them are almost impassable. The only road that looks like a turnpike is to Selkirk; but even it in many places is so deep, as greatly to obstruct travelling. The distance is about 16 miles, and it requires four hours to ride it. The snow also, at times, is a great inconvenience; often for many months, we can have no intercourse with mankind. . . . Another great disadvantage is the want of bridges. . . . In this parish there are 12 ploughs, and 20 carts, but no carriages."[9] Hogg himself surveys his native county in "Statistics of Selkirkshire" in 1832, concentrating more on such physical details as the two lakes of unsurpassable beauty, St. Mary's Loch and the Loch of the Lowes, in contrast to the nine ugly lakes in the south-east (filled with voracious pike which make the trout fishing poor), and the 30,000 sheep, than on the sparsely inhabited parishes of Ettrick and Yarrow and towns of Selkirk and Galashiels.[10]

Hogg soon came to know the country through the hardships and beauties of a shepherd's life, for at age six his formal education at the parish schoolhouse ended with the bankruptcy of his father. In his autobiography, he tells how he "was hired by a farmer in the neighborhood to herd a few cows; my wages for the half year being a ewe lamb and a pair of new shoes." Later, his parents put him to school with a boy who was teaching a neighbor farmer's children, and he advanced to the class which read in the Bible, but he never mastered handwriting. "Thus terminated my education. After this I was never another day at any school whatever. In all I had spent about half a year at it. . . . I was again, that very spring, sent away to my old occupation of herding cows. This employment, the worst and lowest known in our country, I was engaged in for several years under sundry masters, till at length I got into the more honourable one of keeping sheep" (*Mem*, 5-6).

This happy promotion occurred sometime before his fourteenth year, and he remained in service as a shepherd until the age of thirty. Most of this time he spent in the hard labor of a solitary life, with only the occasional diversions of games at market days and races with other shepherds. "I neither read nor wrote," he recounts; "nor had I access to any book save the Bible. I was greatly taken with our version of the Psalms of David, learned the most of them by heart, and have a great partiality for them unto this day" (*Mem*, 7). His only artistic endeavor during the early years of his shepherding days occurred when he saved five shillings of his wages and bought an old violin with which he "generally spent an hour or two every night in sawing over my favourite old Scottish tunes; and my bed being always in stables and cow-houses, I disturbed nobody but myself and my associate quad-rupeds, whom I believed to be greatly delighted with my strains. At all events they never complained, which the biped part of my neighbours did frequently, to my pity and utter indignation" (*Mem*, 7). This early interest in melody suggests the excellence of Hogg's ear—he apparently taught himself the violin—and pre-pared the way for his later songs, varied in their metres but always closely and deliberately tied to melody, like the old ballads and songs to be sung and not read.

At the age of twenty, Hogg entered the service of Mr. Laidlaw of Blackhouse and over the next ten years became intimate with the family, especially with the son William, later Scott's amanuen-sis; they encouraged Hogg to use their well-stocked and modern library. Earlier, Hogg had become acquainted with Blind Harry's "Life and Adventures of Sir William Wallace" and Allan Ram-say's "Gentle Shepherd," but he "could not help regretting deeply that they were not in prose, that every body might have understood them. . . . I made exceedingly slow progress in reading them. The little reading that I had learned I had nearly lost, and the Scottish dialect quite confounded me; so that, before I got to the end of a line, I had commonly lost the rhyme of the preceding one" (*Mem*, 8). Now, under the influence of the books in Laid-law's house and with a subscription to a circulating library at nearby Peebles, Hogg began to compose his own verses: "For several years my compositions consisted wholly of songs and ballads made up for the lasses to sing in chorus; and a proud man I was when I first heard the rosy nymphs chaunting my uncouth strains, and jeering me by the still dear appellation of 'Jamie the poeter' " (*Mem*, 10).

Writing, however, was another problem, for he had to teach himself again: "I had no method of learning to write, save by following the Italian alphabet; and though I always stripped myself of coat and vest when I began to pen a song, yet my wrist took a cramp, so that I could rarely make above four or six lines at a sitting. . . . Having very little spare time from my flock, which was unruly enough, I folded and stitched a few sheets of paper, which I carried in my pocket. I had no inkhorn; but, in place of it, I borrowed a small vial, which I fixed in a hole in the breast of my waistcoat; and having a cork fastened by a piece of twine, it answered the purpose fully as well. Thus equipped, whenever a leisure minute or two offered, and I had nothing else to do, I sat down and wrote out my thoughts as I found them. This is still my invariable practice in writing prose" (*Mem*, 10-11). This method, which seems indeed to have stayed with him throughout his life, accounts for many of the structural difficulties to be found in even the best of his stories: abrupt endings, unanswered questions, undeveloped characters, and lack of logic and coherence.

Poetry, on the other hand, Hogg composed wholly in his head, or on a slate, "ere ever I put pen to paper; and then I write it down as fast as the A, B, C. When once it is written, it remains in that state; it being . . . with the utmost difficulty that I can be brought to alter one syllable, which I think is partly owing to the above practice" (*Mem*, 11). Hogg did rework poems in various editions and surely did not compose his long narratives wholly in his head (although the worst parts of *Mador of the Moor*, for instance, seem the result of his disorganized method of writing prose), but the habit persisted, and Hogg's "slate" became an object of amusement and awe to his Edinburgh friends.

A final story from this period of Hogg's life has been generally accepted by most of his biographers, and whether true or not suggests much of the Shepherd's character. "The first time I ever heard of Burns was in 1797," he writes;

One day during that summer a half daft man, named John Scott, came to me on the hill, and to amuse me repeated Tam O'Shanter. I was delighted! I was far more than delighted—I was ravished! I cannot describe my feelings; but, in short, before Jock Scott left me, I could recite the poem from beginning to end, and it has been my favourite poem ever since. He told me it was made by one Robert Burns, the sweetest poet that ever was born; but that he was now dead, and his place would never be supplied. . . .

This formed a new epoch of my life. Every day I pondered on the genius and fate of Burns. I wept, and always thought with myself—what is to hinder me from succeeding Burns? I too was born on the 25th of

January, and I have much more time to read and compose than any ploughman could have, and can sing more old songs than ever plough-man could in the world. But then I wept again because I could not write. However, I resolved to be a poet. . . . (*Mem*, 11)

Though it seems likely that the Laidlaw library would have included Burns, and that his songs would have been known even in the isolated parishes of Ettrick and Yarrow, there can be no doubt of Hogg's tremendous response to Burns's work. He reacted first to the form and music of the songs, and many of his most conventional lyrics resemble, at least superficially, his brother poet's songs. On a deeper level, however, Hogg would find much in the humor and burlesque of the comic pieces and in the irony of the satires.

At the time, however, the Shepherd needed only inspiration, and with the example of Burns and the ambition to become his equal, Hogg began contributing pieces to the *Scots Magazine*. In 1800 his patriotic and sprightly war-song "Donald M'Donald" became, according to Hogg's own account, universally accepted. He tells of hearing it sung in a Lancaster theater, with the final stanza having English names substituted for the Scottish clans, and of coming upon a young soldier in Dumfriesshire singing it by himself in the woods and ending "in the height of his enthusiasms, [hoisting] his cap on the end of his staff, and [dancing] it about triumphantly" (*Poems*, 283). The song, however, was more popular than the author's name, for Hogg received no credit as its composer. Such early success led him, though, to publish *Scottish Pastorals*, a poorly printed, sixty-two-page pamphlet on "whitey-brown" paper containing seven poems, only one of which was subsequently reprinted. The volume received little attention, and, though Hogg seemed happy enough with it at the time, mentioning it in his letters, in later years he dismissed it with an involved story of how he made up the copy from memory when in town and had no chance to correct the proofs before publication. Hogg continued to write, even though his main interest was in farming; he planned to take a farm in the Highlands, even writing a "Farewell to Ettrick," but the project fell through, and he returned to his shepherd's trade and to odd jobs for the next years.

In 1802, however, he had met Walter Scott, collecting new material for his expanded *Minstrelsy of the Scottish Border*, the first edition of which had just appeared. Hogg had already sent Scott, through Laidlaw, transcriptions of old ballads taken from his mother's singing, and that summer he took the two men to hear her in person. Delighted with her recital, Scott asked her whether it had ever been in print; "Oo, na, na, sir, it was never printed i' the world, for my brothers an' me learned it frae auld Andrew Moor, an' he learned it, an' mony mae, frae auld Baby Mettlin, that was housekeeper to the first laird o' Tushilaw. . . . Except George Warton and James Steward, there was never ane o' my sangs prentit till ye prentit them yoursell, an' ye hae spoilt them a'thegither. They war made for singing, an' no for reading; and they're nouther right spelled nor right setten down" (*Mem*, 61-62).[11] The rest of Scott's visit passed in viewing the countryside and talking and drinking around the fireside. Scott later used part of the talk, an anecdote about the difference between long and short sheep, in *The Black Dwarf* and thus gave Hogg the clue to the identity of the anonymous author of the Waverley novels.

The meeting began a long friendship that lasted until Scott's death. Scott acted as Hogg's friend and adviser, and encouraged and supported him even above the generous aid which the Wizard of the North gave those who petitioned him. Hogg dedicated his first important volume of poems to Scott, imitated him, parodied him, revised and edited according to his advice, and idolized him. In *The Queen's Wake*, Scott successfully tunes the ancient minstrel's harp of Ettrick which had lain lost since presented by Mary Queen of Scots so that once again Border chiefs and fairies respond to the "magic strain." The poem's conclusion sums up the influence of both Scott and Hogg's mother:

> Blest be his generous heart for aye!
> He told me where the relic lay;
> Pointed my way with ready will,
> Afar on Ettrick's wildest hill;
> Watched my first notes with curious eye,
> And wondered at my minstrelsy:
> He little weened a parent's tongue
> Such strains had o'er my cradle sung.
>
> (*Poems*, 58)

The poet had been formed; now he need only gain an audience.

## II   *Writer of Edinburgh*

Despite the publication in 1807 of both *The Mountain Bard* and
*The Shepherd's Guide*, a treatise on the diseases of sheep, the
years from 1800 to 1810 were disastrous for Hogg. An attempt to
farm in the Highlands collapsed, and the £300 from the two
volumes disappeared when he blundered into bad deals over
another two farms. These business failures so colored his reputation that he couldn't even find work as a shepherd in Ettrick, and
he had no success as a kind of land assessor. "For a whole
winter," he writes, "I found myself without employment, and
without money, in my native country; therefore, in February
1810, in utter desperation, I took my plaid about my shoulders,
and marched away to Edinburgh, determined, since no better
could be, to push my fortune as a literary man" (*Mem*, 18). He
was in his fortieth year, the author of only two small volumes of
verse, but he had the ambition, naiveté, and enthusiasm of a man
half his age.

However, "on going to Edinburgh, I found that my poetical
talents were rated nearly as low there as my shepherd qualities
were in Ettrick," Hogg writes (*Mem*, 18). Nevertheless, he
managed to persuade Archibald Constable, the publisher of
*Mountain Bard* who "had a sort of kindness for me" (19), to put
out another book of poems, *The Forest Minstrel*; but this collection, too, brought him neither fame nor money. So Hogg planned
something characteristically outrageous: the editing, writing, and
publishing of a weekly paper modeled on Addison and Steele's
*Spectator*. "All this time I had never been once in any polished
society—had read next to nothing—was now in the 38th [40th]
year of my age—and knew no more of human life or manners
than a child. I was a sort of natural songster, without another
advantage on earth" (19). Scott, astonished by Hogg's presump-
tion in claiming his papers would be more original than his predecessors', finally agreed, commenting, "Yes they will certainly be
original enough with a vengeance" (*FA*, 115).

*The Spy* appeared on Saturday, September 1, 1810, and the
most remarkable thing about the entire venture is that he was able
to sustain it for a full year. It might even have flourished—it
included the first appearances of many of his tales and poems
which would later be reprinted and expanded—had not Hogg

chosen to continue a slightly bawdy story begun in the third number and had not the first printer been more devoted to the pub than to his profession. The enterprise came to an end, however, when a lack of subscribers forced Hogg to write a "Farewell Paper" on September 17, 1811, in which he cast aside the persona of a sixty-year-old bachelor observer of manners to speak in his own voice about false friends, squeamish readers, and foolish critics who lacked sympathy for a harsh and unpolished style despite the laudable sentiments expressed. In any event, he suggests, "Thus far may be said in justification of those papers, that in no one instance is the cause of religion, virtue, or benevolence injured or violated, but always encouraged, however ineffectively; therefore, though the Spy merits not admiration, he is at least entitled to kindness for his good intentions."[12] For all those good intentions, though, Hogg again found himself out of a job.

For the next year and a half, Hogg was literally kept from starving by two merchants, John Grieve and Henry Scott, who provided him with food and clothing. At the same time, he became involved with the "Forum," a literary and debating society formed by several young men of the town. Appointed secretary with a salary of £20 per year that he claimed was never paid, Hogg spoke once or twice at every weekly public meeting. He credits this "discerning public" as being a major factor in his literary education, since "the smallest departure from good taste, or from the question, was sure to draw down disapproval, [whereas] no good saying ever missed observation and applause" (*Mem*, 23). Hogg overstates the influence, however, for though he may have appreciated the applause, he rarely worried about digressions or lapses of taste in his works.

Narrative poetry being then in vogue, due to the enormous popularity of Byron's *Childe Harold* and Scott's *Lady of the Lake* and *Marmion*, Grieve suggested that Hogg return to his poetic endeavors. The Shepherd took some ballads and metrical romances which he had already written, added a frame-story involving a poetic competition in honor of the return to Scotland of Queen Mary, and set off to find a publisher. But only Grieve would listen seriously to the poem; Constable finally offered Hogg £100 if he could procure two hundred subscribers. Though his friends did secure them, Hogg turned the manuscript over to George Goldie, a young bookseller whom he had met at the Forum, and who offered better terms. *The Queen's Wake*, which made Hogg's reputation, appeared in the spring of 1813.

Like Byron, Hogg awoke to find himself famous, at least in Edinburgh literary circles. The first fearfully awaited reaction came from William Dunlop, an Ettrick wine merchant, who said, on seeing Hogg: "Ye useless poetical deevil that ye're! What hae ye been doing a' this time?"—"What doing, Willie! what do you mean?"—"D--n your stupid head, ye hae been pestering us wi' four-penny papers an' daft shilly-shally sangs, an' bletherin' an' speakin' i' the Forum, an' yet had stuff in ye to produce a thing like this!"—"Ay, Willie," said Hogg; "have you seen my new beuk?"—"Ay, faith, that I have, man; and it has lickit me out o' a night's sleep. Ye hae hit the right nail on the head now. Yon 's the very thing, sir" (*Mem*, 26). Containing two of Hogg's acknowledged classics, "Kilmeny" and "The Witch of Fife," along with some respectable narratives and an interesting frame-tale, *The Queen's Wake* went through six editions in the next six years and two more after Hogg's death. The success, which confirmed his belief in his powers, made him an established literary figure. From then on, Grieve and Scott had to share the Shepherd's dinner-table company with the hostesses of literary suppers. Hogg met the rising John Wilson, author of *The Isle of Palms*, and, after Goldie's bankruptcy, made contact with William Blackwood, who would become one of the dominant literary publishers in Edinburgh and with whom Hogg would be involved for the rest of his career.

Following the success of the *Wake*, Hogg became extremely prolific. A visit to the Highlands led to the writing of *Mador of the Moor*, a narrative in Spenserian stanzas which suffers from comparison with its model, *The Lady of the Lake*. Upon his return, he wrote the strange, underrated dream-vision *Pilgrims of the Sun*, his most original, if not totally successful, narrative poem, in which he attempted more profound themes than he ever would again. His next project he himself described as extravagant: a collection of original poems from the chief living poets of Britain, to be edited by himself and printed in an elegant volume. Accordingly, he contacted Byron, Scott, Wordsworth, Southey, Wilson, and others to solicit material. Some of the minor poets sent pieces, but only Wordsworth, of the major writers, sent anything; Byron promised a poem (Hogg thought it was "Lara") but never sent it, and Scott declined—a refusal that initiated their only serious quarrel[13]—saying that he thought it not right that a man should live by the labor of others. Without the important contributors, Hogg knew the book would fail, so he returned the poems he had received; but then another idea occurred to him: retaining the same format, *he* would write the poems in imitation of his contemporaries. An accomplished poet whose strength was his ear and who had already written several ballad imitations, he found the task easy, claiming to have written the book in three weeks. Thus, in 1816, appeared *The Poetic Mirror, or, The Living Bards of Britain*, edited anonymously and containing, apparently, poems by Wordsworth, Byron, Scott, Hogg, Coleridge, Southey, and Wilson. These superb parodies represent one of Hogg's major achievements.

The following year Hogg published his *Dramatic Tales*, consisting of four verse dramas, but except for an occasional scene among peasants or fairies, they prove only that Hogg had no talent whatever for drama. At the same time, Blackwood started *Blackwood's Magazine*, largely as a Tory reply to Constable's *Edinburgh Magazine*. When Blackwood's original editors, Thomas Pringle and James Cleghorn, fell out with the publisher and joined Constable, Hogg and the new editors, John Gibson Lockhart and Wilson, wrote the scathing "Chaldee Manuscript," an allegorical account of the feud which was so scandalous that it had to be withdrawn from later editions and bound volumes of the magazine; but its notoriety got the journal off to a contentious start.[14] From the first issue until his death, except for times when he quarreled with Blackwood, Hogg was one of "Maga's" principal contributors, providing almost a hundred pieces. In addition, of course, he also figured as the central character, in both senses of the word, of Wilson's *Noctes Ambrosianae*.

By the time *Blackwood's* was fairly launched, however, Hogg had left Edinburgh for Ettrick, where he would spend the rest of his life. The Shepherd had dedicated *The Forest Minstrel* to the Duchess of Buccleuch, and after her death, the Duke followed her wishes and granted Hogg the farm of Altrive Lake for a rent so nominal that it was never recorded. After a house was built and the farm stocked, with Hogg commuting between city and country, the Shepherd happily, and no doubt thankfully, left the young, high-powered literati of Edinburgh and returned to the place of his youth. His talent continued to be recognized, his stories and poems to be sought, and his reputation to grow.

### III   *Author of Altrive Lake*

The move to Altrive did not lessen Hogg's productivity. In 1818 he published his first novel, *The Brownie of Bodsbeck*, his best historical work and among the most coherent of his long fictions. Set in the days of the Covenanters, the short novel suffered from its resemblance to Scott's *Old Mortality*, although the two books differ considerably. The next year Hogg published the first volume of *Jacobite Relics*, his collection of Highland songs and music on the model of Scott's *Minstrelsy*. Hogg's limited knowledge of history, however, and his freedom with facts make the *Relics* unsuitable for significant scholarly use. The preservation of some of the melodies and a revised wording of "Charlie is my Darling" remain the Shepherd's contributions to Highland minstrelsy. In 1820 his first collection of fiction, *Winter Evening Tales*, appeared, stories reprinted and revised from *The Spy* and *Blackwood's*. A revised version of the *Memoir* states with justifiable pride: "The following list of works may appear trifling in the eyes of some, but when it is considered that they have been produced by a man almost devoid of education, and principally, in his early days, debarred from every advantage in life, and possessed only of a quick eye in observing the operations of nature, it is certainly a sufficient excuse for inserting them here. . . . I was forty [actually forty-two] years of age before I wrote the 'Queen's Wake.' That poem was published in 1813; so that in that and the next six years I wrote and published . . . fifteen volumes in seven years, besides many articles . . ." (*Mem*, 50-51).

In his fiftieth year, after a circumspect ten-year courtship, the Shepherd married Margaret Phillips, twenty years his junior, the daughter of a well-to-do farmer. Shortly thereafter he again overextended his financial resources by leasing a nearby farm at Mount Benger which had already ruined two men more capable than Hogg in farming affairs. The failure of his father-in-law, from whom he had expected help, also hampered his ventures, so that more and more he turned to writing as a major source of income. Besides writing for *Blackwood's*, he published three novels in three years—*The Three Perils of Man*, an historical romance of war and witchcraft; *The Three Perils of Woman*, a domestic novel of manners; and *The Private Memoirs and Confessions of a Justified Sinner*, the account of a religious zealot. In 1825 he completed the epic poem *Queen Hynde*, the weakest of his long poetical works.

Financial problems continued to plague Hogg, for managing the two farms began to be more than he could handle. In addition, his reputation brought a constant flow of visitors whom the good-natured Hoggs would not turn away without meals or even overnight accommodation, a further drain on finances as well as writing time. Scott had invited Hogg to London to attend the coronation of George IV, in hopes that a poem might catch the royal favor, but Hogg replied that he couldn't miss the St. Boswell's Fair and had to decline. Scott treated the affair as a joke—that Hogg should miss the coronation for a county fair[15]—and continued to press for a pension for the Shepherd from the Royal Literary Society. When King George came to Edinburgh, Hogg did write a masque, "The Royal Jubilee," which produced a letter from Robert Peel but no pension. Other such attempts also failed, so Hogg continued to depend on his literary income. He contributed, for example, to annuals, lavishly produced books designed as gifts for the young, but often ran into difficulties of taste. Mrs. S. C. Hall, in rejecting a tale "interesting and powerfully written," wrote: "Surely, my dear sir, you would not wish my young readers to credit supernatural appearances? I could not take it upon my conscience to send the little darlings tremblingly to bed after perusing the very perfection of ghost stories from your pen. I find it singularly perplexing that the first tale you send me was one of seduction, your second (a thing by the way of extraordinary spirit and beauty) was a wanderer from fairy land. . . . Pray, pray write me a simple tale, telling about your own pure and immortal Scottish children—without love—or ghosts—or fairies."[16]

In an attempt to provide financial security for his family, Hogg went to London in 1832—his first visit—to arrange for the publication of the *Altrive Tales*, a twelve-volume edition of his prose in the same handsome format as Scott's Waverley novels. After an expensive and arduous journey for a man in his sixties—involving a nine-day trip by packet from Edinburgh to London—Hogg arrived in the capital lonesome for his wife and five children.

But he was taken up by the literary society, invited to dinners, and generally made much of. The highlight of the visit was a huge dinner, given on Burns's birthday but dedicated to the recognition of Hogg. He wrote his wife: "General Sir John Malcolm was in the chair, and acquitted himself only too well. I was on his right hand and supported by two lords, four baronets, and a whole row of generals, chiefs of clans and all the literature of the Metropolis. I was the hero of the evening, and every gentleman and nobleman ended with some encomiums of me, Lockhart in particular abounded with them."[17] Hogg later wrote of his London adventure: "Such flummery I never saw in this world. . . . I am quite sick of it. You know I was always fond of flattery and approbation, but I have at length lived to be overpowered with it."[18] Unfortunately, though, the business side of his trip was unsuccessful, since the publisher, James Cochrane, went bankrupt and only one volume of *Altrive Tales* appeared.

In that same year, Sir Walter Scott died. The two men had last met at the Gordon Arms inn on Hogg's farm, when Scott sent word that he would be passing but was too ill to make the extra trip to Altrive. With Scott leaning on Hogg's shoulder throughout their walk, they "talked of many things past present and to come but both [Scott's] memory and onward calculation appeared to me then to be considerably decayed. . . . He often changed the subject very abruptly and never laughed. He expressed the deepest concern for my welfare and success . . . and all mixed with sorrow for my worldly misfortunes. There is little doubt that his own were then preying on his vitals" (*FA*, 133). Two years after Scott's death, Hogg wrote the *Familiar Anecdotes of Sir Walter Scott*, which contained the preceding description along with several controversial passages.

Also in 1834 appeared the *Lay Sermons*, a series of moralistic and pious essays in a free and familiar style. Hogg's final effort was a three-volume collection of *Tales of the Wars of Montrose* which he again entrusted to Cochrane who again failed, so that when the Shepherd died of jaundice, his family was left without any significant income. Collections of his poems and tales appeared in the next couple of years, along with an undistinguished edition of Burns's poems to which Hogg had contributed some notes and a life of the poet largely taken from Lockhart's earlier biography. Hogg was as unlucky in the promoters of his reputation after his death as he had often been in his publishers during his life. Wilson promised to write a full biography, but never did, and, according to the family, he even lost many of the personal papers and manuscripts which had been given him. And Lockhart, angry and unfair, was to have almost the last word when he wrote in his *Life of Scott* that Hogg "died on the 21st of November 1835;—but it had been better for his fame had his end been of earlier date, for he did not follow his best benefactor until he had insulted his dust."[19] Hogg's daughter tried to correct this final picture, and that of the Shepherd of the *Noctes*, in her *Memorials of James Hogg* in 1885, and his local fame was preserved by an impressive statue set on the hill overlooking St. Mary's Loch, about which the sheep still graze. The most noteworthy contemporary tribute came in the "Extempore Effusion Upon the Death of James Hogg," in which Wordsworth lamented the deaths of Scott, Hogg, Coleridge, and Crabbe.[20] Egotistic, ambitious, naive, good-natured, a lover of life, Hogg remains an extraordinary man and writer in an age moving quickly away from the life he knew. His death marked the passing, surely, of one of the last self-taught geniuses, a writer not of the people as Burns had been, but of the people's traditions.

CHAPTER 2

# Nonfiction Works

H OGG'S nonfiction ranges from informal autobiography and
biography to essays and tracts, letters, historical notes,
sermons, and sketches of nature, character, and pastoral life; they
illustrate both the important concerns and the techniques found in
his poetry and fiction as well. Perhaps most important to an
understanding of Hogg's writing, after the factual material of his
life, are the methods of narration—the tone, the personae, the
details of observation—which mark his nonfiction efforts. As the
nonfiction merges with the fiction, and often with the poetry, his
chief realistic effects can be traced to his autobiographical techniques. Moreover, the three important works of nonfiction—the
*Memoir*, the *Shepherd's Calendar*, and the *Familiar Anecdotes*—
constitute a significant body of Hogg's work, and demand attention in their own right.

## I Memoir of the Author's Life

"I like to write about myself: in fact, there are few things which
I like better. . . . [In] this *important* Memoir, now to be brought
forward for the fourth time, at different periods of my life, I shall
narrate with the same frankness as formerly; and in all, relating
either to others or myself, speak fearlessly and unreservedly out"
(*Mem*, 3). Thus Hogg begins the final version of an autobiography
that had been published in 1807, 1821, and now in 1832 as the
preface to the *Altrive Tales*. He usually made only additions and
slight changes in the various editions, so the characters and events
remain fairly consistent.[1] Obviously Hogg wished to set forth his
intriguing background to stimulate the sale of his poetry. The first

version begins with a letter from Scott which comments on "the efforts of a strong mind and vigorous imagination, to develop themselves even under the most disadvantageous circumstances, [that] may be always considered with pleasure, and often with profit" (*Mem*, 5). Even in the final edition, Hogg prefaces Scott's letter with a note saying that his life seems "much more of a romance than mere fancy could have suggested" (*Mem*, 3). In this document, as in the other autobiographical writings, character remains the chief interest—Hogg's perception of himself and his observations of others. Even the way in which he presents those observations reveals his character.

Hogg can hardly be called a great stylist. Often careless about words,[2] he was basically a storyteller of the oral tradition, and, like Scott, his prose often reads better aloud. The tone of the *Memoir*, indeed of almost all his writing, reflects his informality. The Shepherd makes an immediate contact with the audience to set up the relationship of speaker and listener. Hence the opening —his enjoyment in writing about himself, his limits, beliefs, justifications for taking the reader's time, and promises (repeated in the tales) of complete honesty and fidelity to fact. This frame relationship, if so it may be called, becomes codified in the device of treating the entire work as a letter to Scott. The letter form often occurs later to introduce and authenticate a magazine tale, as does the overt storytelling technique in many of his frame situations.

Another aspect of this informal approach occurs in Hogg's organization of the material. Though autobiography usually has a simple narrative form, Hogg's *Memoir* continually jumps from point to point. Events occur in the first part in proper time sequence, but Hogg quite casually breaks the chronology, as when he mentions Byron's promise to contribute to the *Poetic Mirror*, then tells of having lost all Byron's letters, and further digresses on the poet's last letter before returning to his original story. He refers briefly to his estrangement from Scott, but the reconciliation does not appear until after a discussion of the *Brownie*, by which time the quarrel had long been made up. Many passages found in the later editions were clearly not added in chronological order; in fact, when the time comes to bring the volume up to date in 1832, Hogg apologizes: "I must now proceed with my reminiscences at random, as from the time the last journal was finished and published I ceased keeping any notes" (*Mem*, 52). This last section, subtitled "Reminiscences of Former Days," consists of a brief narrative of events and publications up to 1831, and concludes with a series of recollections of literary characters—Scott, Southey, Wordsworth, Galt, and Lockhart, among others—whom he had treated only briefly, if at all, in their chronological place.

This emphasis on reminiscence marks another of the idiosyncrasies of the *Memoir*, its inaccuracy or incompleteness. Hogg's misdating of his own birth has already been mentioned; other inaccuracies derive from faulty memory about dates, but many of them also serve to heighten character, not always to the author's credit. The quarrel with Scott, for example, surely one time when the Shepherd comes off badly, is extended in time to over a year rather than the actual few months. Hogg also leaves out several personal events that might have been of interest. Only concerned with writing a literary biography, for example, Hogg mentions his wife but once, and cheerfully disposes of his entire married life as "so uniformly smooth and happy [that] I cannot distinguish one part from another, save by some remarkably good days of fishing, shooting, and curling on the ice" (*Mem*, 54). Yet even of those days, and of the celebrated "literary" discussions with Wilson and other literati at Tibbie Shiels's famous inn on the shores of St. Mary's Loch, there is no mention. Hogg's lack of concern for accuracy also leads him to deliberately blur the distinctions between fact and fiction: "Those who desire to peruse my youthful love adventures," he advises, "will find some of the best of them in those of 'George Cochrane' in the [*Altrive Tales*]" (*Mem*, 54).

The carelessness about facts, the inconsistent chronological organization, and the storyteller's pose all suggest the informality of the Shepherd's nature, an easiness and good fellowship apparently reflected in his private life.[3] But they also suggest his chief approach, for above all, Hogg worked in anecdotes. Like the old ballads, Hogg's pieces come alive in the single incident, where character is portrayed or scenery described, where two characters interact with one another. Over the long haul of a novel or narrative poem, his imagination breaks down, his consistency falters, his emphasis changes, as another incident, which perhaps demands its own treatment, engages his interest. Hence, in the autobiographies, some of the best parts involve just such scenes: the first meeting with Scott and the reaction of Hogg's mother, the meeting with William Dunlop after the publication of *The Queen's Wake*, the discussions with Constable and Blackwood, and the memories of Scott, Southey, and Wordsworth. Too, because he need not invent incidents, the *Memoir* and the *Familiar Anecdotes* still stand, for all their chronological wandering, among the most coherent of Hogg's works. Freed from the necessity of contriving the action, Hogg can focus on the self-portrait at the center of both books.

He represents his most admirable qualities as honesty and frankness. Indeed, Hogg begins by saying he "shall tell the plain truth, and nothing but the truth" (*Mem*, 3). With but few exceptions, he carries out this promise with regard to himself. Although he naturally tries to justify certain of his quarrels with publishers—and in many cases it is easy to sympathize with his side, even though he may have been wrong[4]—he rarely presents himself or his actions dishonestly. Often he shows himself at his worst, as in the quarrel with Scott, which he describes as "an anecdote which I must relate, though with little credit to myself" (*Mem*, 47). Usually, however, this frankness serves a comic purpose, as he himself becomes the butt of a joke. In agreeing to meet a Mr. Wordsworth, Hogg recalls that "not having the least conception that the great poet of the Lakes was in Edinburgh, . . . I took it for the celebrated horse-dealer of the same name, and entertained some shrewd misgivings, how he should chance to be a guest in a house where only the first people in Edinburgh were wont to be invited." Assured that Wordsworth is "exceedingly intelligent" even though he "proses a little," Hogg replies, "I dare say he is; at all events, he is allowed to be a good judge of horse-flesh!" The joke continues for some time, and Hogg later notes the same mistake being made by people the two poets meet in their tour of Yarrow, gentlemen "expressing themselves as at a loss why I should be travelling the country with a *horse-couper*" (*Mem*, 68).

Also evident throughout the book is Hogg's pride in his achievements. Less charitable commentators refer to his ambition and egotism,[5] though evidently Hogg's pride was not simply considerable but justifiable as well. How many writers, Hogg implies throughout, with but six months of school and unable to read or write until twenty, could boast of fifteen volumes in seven years, thirty volumes in a lifetime? Moreover, how many people of

Hogg's background could boast of personal friendships with the leading literary men of the day? Rarely in the course of the recollections does Hogg display any sense of social inferiority by striving to climb higher or by trying to live down his background. In fact, he points out his acceptance by all levels of society; as he comments proudly in *Lay Sermons*, "For upwards of twenty years I have mixed with all classes of society, and as I never knew to which I belonged, I have been perfectly free and at my ease in them all."[6]

The social acceptance came from Hogg's good-natured conviviality, an attribute almost legendary among his friends. Hogg portrays himself as a good companion, though not the hard-drinking, Falstaffian buffoon of the *Noctes*. Drink, however, is a natural boon to fellowship, perhaps even to creativity, as Hogg notes in his reminiscence of Southey: "I sent a note up to Greta Hall, requesting him to come down and see me, and drink one half mutchkin along with me. He came on the instant, and stayed with me about an hour and a half. But I was a grieved as well as an astonished man, when I found that he refused all participation in my beverage of rum punch. For a poet to refuse his glass was to me a phenomenon; and I confess I doubted in my own mind, and doubt to this day, if perfect sobriety and transcendent poetical genius can exist together. In Scotland I am sure they cannot. With regard to the English, I shall leave them to settle that among themselves, as they have little that is worth drinking" (*Mem*, 67). The printer of *The Spy*, Hogg notes, "loved a joke and a dram. He sent for me every day about one o'clock, to consult about the publication; and then we uniformly went down to a dark house in the Cowgate, where we drank whisky and ate rolls with a number of printers, the dirtiest and leanest-looking men I had ever seen." In this instance, however, the liquor gets hold of him and he sees himself "going straight to the devil," so he determines to change publishers (*Mem*, 20-21). This episode is one of the few instances of moralizing in the *Memoir*; and although many later works contain specific moral strictures, rarely does he condemn drinking.

Generally, Hogg's good nature never leaves him, despite enormous trials, since his life—both literary and agricultural—can be seen as a series of disasters. His publishers went bankrupt, his name appeared on articles he hadn't written, his character was portrayed inaccurately and insultingly; his farms failed due to poor management, bad luck, and victimization by dishonest or insolvent operators. At the end of his life he found himself with no money and five children, having to start over at the age of sixty. Yet he says, "It will be consolatory however to my friends to be assured that none of these reverses ever preyed in the smallest degree on my spirits. As long as I did all for the best, and was conscious that no man could ever accuse me of dishonesty, I laughed at the futility of my own calculations, and let my earnings go as they came, amid contentment and happiness, determined to make more money as soon as possible, although it should go the same way." "One may think," he continues, "that I must have worn out a life of misery and wretchedness; but the case has been quite the reverse. I never knew either man or woman who has been so uniformly happy as I have been; which has been partly owing to a good constitution, and partly from the conviction that a heavenly gift, conferring the powers of immortal song, was inherent in my soul" (*Mem*, 54). Despite his misfortunes, no bitterness shows in his recollections.[7]

What emerges from the *Memoir*, then, is the picture of a companionable, cheerful, innocent, content, and genuinely gifted man of the people. His virtues are those of the country: frankness, honesty, forgiveness, pride of accomplishment, hospitality, genial good nature. Likewise, his faults are those often connected with rural dwellers: short temper, lack of sophistication, simplicity, impatience with city life. His pleasures also reflect the simple life: drinking, fishing, walking, reading poetry, talking to friends. Though he gives few details of his private life—even had such been appropriate in nineteenth-century autobiography—his account remains fairly consistent with the image presented in his letters and in the portraits by his contemporaries.[8] There can be little doubt of Hogg's openness, cheerfulness, and lack of sophistication and intellectualism; he was an enjoyer of life, not a profound thinker.

The importance of the Hogg of the *Memoir*, besides its being an autobiographical achievement of consequence—a picture of a happy man—lies in its usefulness as a guide to Hogg's other uses of persona. (It, of course, must be distinguished from other portraits of "Hogg" as well: in the *Noctes* or such oddities as the anonymous "A Day in Kent," wherein a group of travelers encounter a Scot carrying a fishing rod and basket, who offers "a draught from a large leather bottle, having first himself, to shew the contents were not poison, partaken largely of the crystal fluid which lay within."⁹) The fact remains that the greater part of Hogg's works occur in the autobiographical mode: many of the long stories, especially, are Defoe-like narratives, and often the frame stories contain narrators who could be Hogg. At the end of the *Confessions*, Hogg even borrows from Wilson and sends the anonymous Editor of the novel to the country where he meets Hogg, a taciturn, Scots-speaking sheep dealer. Autobiography, real and fictional, remains crucial for Hogg in giving verisimilitude to even the most incredible of tales.

## II  *Sketches and* The Shepherd's Calendar

The *Memoir* deals primarily with Hogg's literary life; his experiences as a shepherd, however, find expression in many sketches throughout his career. "Tales and Anecdotes of the Pastoral Life" began in the first issue of *Blackwood's*, and other sketches appeared from time to time in the next years; later the series gained the formal title of "The Shepherd's Calendar" and continued, with various subsections and categories—including stories—for nine years until being slightly revised and collected in book form in 1829. Although Hogg usually narrates these sketches himself, he often shifts attention away from his own character to focus on the anecdote at the heart of the piece. These sketches form a companion-piece to the *Memoir* and again show many of Hogg's characteristic narrative techniques; completely readable, they provide additional interest in their presentation of a life and time unfamiliar to much of the world and now largely irrecoverable.

Among the most interesting of these pieces, the ones based on Hogg's experiences as a shepherd show his capacity for observing and recreating a natural setting and event. Most follow the pattern of a series of anecdotes or incidents grouped around a main subject. "Storms," for instance, opens with the information that shepherds place less reliance on calendar dates than on events: "Storms constitute the various eras of the pastoral life. They are the red lines in the shepherd's manual—the remembrancers of years and ages that are past—the tablets of memory by which the ages of his children, the times of his ancestors, and the rise and downfall of families, are invariably ascertained" (*Tales*, 140).

Hogg then details two famous seventeenth-century snowstorms, before mentioning the major storms of the past century and then the primary incident of this sketch, the devastating storm of January 24, 1794. He begins with figures: seventeen shepherds dead, with upwards of thirty carried home insensible, "but the number of sheep that were lost far outwent any possibility of calculation. One farmer alone, Mr. Thomas Beattie, lost seventy-two scores for his own share; and many others, in the same quarter, from thirty to forty scores each" (141).

Then the Shepherd turns to personal experience. First he verifies the size of the disaster with specific details that go beyond mere statistics: "Whole flocks," he writes, "were overwhelmed with snow, and no one ever knew where they were till the snow was dissolved, when they were all found dead. I myself witnessed one particular instance of this on the farm of Thickside; there were twelve scores of excellent ewes, all one age, that were missing there all the time that the snow lay, which was only a week, and no traces of them could be found; when the snow went away, they were discovered all lying dead, with their heads one way, as if a flock of sheep had dropped dead going from the washing" (141). Finally, Hogg tells of journeying to a meeting of a "sort of literary society" of shepherds to be held at a remote farm. He describes the beginnings of the storm, the various calms and winds, light snows, and frosts. As the storm worsens, he turns back for his sheep; after saving most of them, he goes off on his own and becomes lost in land now covered with snow that changes the landscape and treacherously covers the river. As the climax, Hogg recreates the disaster by relating it in terms of human consciousness. "I could find no water," he says,

and began to dread that for all my accuracy I had gone wrong. I was greatly astonished; and standing still to consider, I looked up towards heaven, I shall not say for what cause, and to my utter amazement thought I beheld trees over my head flourishing abroad over the whole sky. I never had seen such an optical delusion before; it was so like enchantment that I knew not what to think, but dreaded that some extra-ordinary thing was coming over me, and that I was deprived of my right senses. I remember I thought the storm was a great judgment sent on us for our sins, and that this strange phantasy was connected with it, an illusion effected by evil spirits. I stood a good while in this painful stance; at length, on making a bold exertion to escape from the fairy vision I came all at once in contact with the old tower. Never in my life did I experience such a relief; I was not only all at once freed from the fairies, but from the dangers of the gorged river. I had come over it on some mountain of snow, I knew not how nor where, nor do I know to this day. . . . Such a day and such a night may the eye of a shepherd never again behold. (144)

The sketch ends with Hogg's account of the popular belief that the storm had come about because of the "literary society" which had indeed met that night and, according to the local people, had raised up the devil, "like a great rough dog at the very time that the tempest began" (147), who could only be bought off by being given one or more of their number. For a time, legal proceedings were considered against those with such demonic intentions.

Many of Hogg's descriptive sketches follow this pattern: thesis, statistics, discussion, personal experience, and, sometimes, a moral tag. His essay on "Sheep," for instance, begins, "The sheep has scarcely any marked character, save that of natural affection, of which it possesses a very great share. It is otherwise a stupid, indifferent animal, having few wants, and fewer expedients" (*Tales*, 402). Then Hogg tells "well authenticated" anecdotes about the "old black-faced" sheep, as opposed to the newer varieties, and finally relates his own experiences in watching ewes standing faithfully over their dead lambs. "It often drew the tears from my eyes," he concludes, "to see her hanging with such fondness over a few bones, mixed with a small portion of wool" (404). In "The Shepherd's Dog," Hogg talks of a famous local breed's facility at gathering sheep; he concludes with the more intimate stories of his own Sirrah, who, besides being an excellent tracker, loved to join the family worship and add his unique voice to the singing of psalms. Hogg also includes anecdotes about "my own renowned Hector," Sirrah's son, with "three times more humour and whim; and though exceedingly docile, his bravest acts were mostly tinctured with a grain of stupidity, which showed his reasoning faculty to be laughably obtuse."[10] Most of the sketches end abruptly; the anecdotes carry the thesis, if indeed the argument be remembered at all. Hogg himself usually seems more interested in telling the story than in pointing the moral, at least in the sketches.

Though Hogg's treatments of animals stress their wondrous

human qualities (including, realistically enough, stupidity and indifference), when he turns to country characters, he looks at their oddities, achieving much of his success through dialogue. The use of the Scots dialect for comic effect is typical of the period—the comic characters of Scott's novels, for instance, usually speak in broad Scots. With eighteenth-century English becoming the language of the upper classes, according to Sydney G. Smith, "English became the medium for expressing 'polite' thoughts, [and] Scots became the medium for more humble expression, chiefly for the jocose, or the bawdy."[11] Hogg makes no special attempt, however, to poke fun at his "Odd Characters" —they are what they are: comic often, but respectable and sincere as well. "Prayers" begins in the habitual way, with a generalization about shepherds: "There is, I believe, no class of men professing the Protestant faith, so truly devout as the shepherds of Scotland. They get all the learning that the parish schools afford; are thoroughly acquainted with the Scriptures; deeply read in theological works, and really, I am sorry to say it, generally much better informed on these topics than their masters. Every shepherd is a man of respectability—he must be so, else he must cease to be a shepherd" (*Tales*, 404). Then come such examples as Adam Scott's prayer of gratitude: "We particularly thank thee for thy great goodness to Meg, and that ever it came into your head to take any thought of sic an useless baw-waw as her" (404). Other prayers show unique phrasings and highly personal references, as in one extempore conclusion to the story of David and Goliath: "And when our besetting sins come bragging and blowstering upon us, like Gully o' Gath, O enable us to fling off the airmer and hairnishin o' the law, whilk we haena proved, and whup up the simple sling o' the gospel, and nail the smooth stanes o' redeeming grace into their foreheads" (405). But the same man's prayer at the burial of his son follows, changing the mood but not the man: "Thou hast seen meet, in thy wise providence, to remove the staff out of my right hand, at the very time when, to us poor sand-blind mortals, it appeared that I stood maist in need o't. But oh it was a sicker ane, and a sure ane, and a dear ane to my heart! and how I'll climb the steep hill o' auld age and sorrow without it, thou mayst ken, but I dinna" (405). Hogg inserts many such prayers in his tales as well, where they help to establish the reality and humanity of the characters.

In another sketch, "Odd Characters," Hogg presents full portraits again through anecdote. He provides no description of Will o' Phaup, his grandfather who had conversed with the fairies; instead, he recounts feats of drinking and racing. Will raced for pints of brandy, for bets made by his master, and for the honor of Scots shepherds against English ones. "His great oath was 'Scots grund!' " says Hogg; "And 'Scots grund, quo' Will o' Phaup,' is a standing exclamation to this day" (*Tales*, 408). Will's skill at running comes in handy when he meets the fairies. One time he followed a pair to a cavern filled with huge old casks, when they turn on him: "The figure that approached him from the cavern was of a gigantic size, with grisly features, and a beard hanging down to his belt. Will did not stop to consider what was best to be done, but, quite forgetting that he was on the face of a hill, almost perpendicular, turned round, and ran with all his might" (410). In the morning the rut Will had made was found in the grass, but no indication of the entrance to the cave. The other two characters in this sketch, Daft Jock Amos and Willie Candlem, are less successful, and the essay, like many of Hogg's pieces, peters out, as if he had started with a good idea but then drifted on without significant or interesting things to add.

Dialect, anecdote, and personal experience, then, are the standard techniques, more important usually than mere description. Even in sketches where one would expect considerable description, as in "Malise's Tour," a fairly conventional Highland travelogue, Hogg emphasizes the personal and the anecdotal. He tells of finding a supposedly lost tomb, only to discover the initials of previous visitors; he does describe some Highland scenery, but then tells of losing his balance and running nearly the whole way downhill (*Spy*, 313-17, 345-50). Three other characteristics, however, have equal importance in the sketches: immediacy of effect, insistence on truth, and (if he has space) an emphasis on moral significance. Hogg gains immediacy again through first-person reporting of experience. In "A Country Funeral," the narrator-observer goes with his father to the funeral of George Mouncie where the scene emerges through the conversation of the mourners; the widow gives the account of her husband's last days as further direct observation. At other times, Hogg shifts tense, even moving from factual to fictional recreation of events, to build his effect. In "Storms," he invents a representative family isolated in a lone glen, left completely to the protection of Heaven: "They have no hope of assistance from man, but are conversant with the Almighty alone. . . . Nothing is to be seen but the conflict of the elements, nor heard but the raving of the storm: then they all kneel around [the shepherd] while he recommends them to the protection of Heaven; and though their little hymn of praise can scarcely be heard even by themselves, as it mixes with the roar of the tempest, they never fail to rise from their devotions with their spirits cheered and their confidence renewed, and go to sleep with an exaltation of mind of which kings and conquerors have no share" (*Tales*, 141).

Hogg ends the above account by commenting, "Often have I been a partaker in such scenes; and never, even in my youngest years, without having my heart deeply impressed by the circumstances," a typical insistence on the truth of the experience. Likewise, George Mouncie's funeral is dated April 10, 1810; Hogg survives the storm of January 24, 1794; old John of the prayers is one of his relatives, Will o' Phaup his grandfather. Hogg uses the same devices to verify his ghost stories: dates, personal experience, letters, tales told to him, even the inclusion of himself and his friends. Hogg's frankness, so emphasized in the *Memoir*, gives the illusion of truth to everything he writes; the tone of sincerity convinces where flat narration would not. Commenting on Will o' Phaup's confrontation with the giant figure, Hogg says, "If the whole of this was an optical delusion, it was the most singular I ever heard or read of. For my part, I do not believe it was; I believe there was such a cavern existing at that day, and that vestiges of it may still be discovered. It was an unfeasible story altogether for a man to invent" (*Tales*, 410). Hogg uses the dating device so consistently that in explaining that the *Lay Sermons* is based on an old manuscript, he states, "I have now given so many tales of *perfect truth* to the public, many of them with not one word of truth in them, that I know I shall not be believed in this."[12] A career of hoaxes necessarily breeds suspicion.

Also evident in these sketches is Hogg's faith in the workings of Providence. Not unduly emphasized but always making itself felt, Hogg's unwavering belief in the power of God underlies all his writings and, like the old songs and stories, is so deeply ingrained in his nature that it becomes a wholly integrated and natural part

of his piece, more moving, perhaps, because of its understate-
ment. In "Storms," Hogg's feeling that the storm "was a great
judgment sent on us for our sins" is echoed by the reactions of
the local people. The representative family trusts in Providence,
alone in their glen; the prayers offered up by peasant patriarchs
resemble Jewish prayers, direct personal appeals to God, comic
often but serious always. The Nature with which the shepherd
becomes familiar is so closely connected to his Creator, that Hogg
can assume that, like the storm family, "we lived, as it were,
inmates of the cloud and the storm; but we stood in a relationship
to the Ruler of these, that neither time nor eternity could ever
cancel. Woe to him that would weaken the bonds with which true
Christianity connects us with Heaven and with each other!"
(*Tales*, 141). Such beliefs, even when directly stated as in this
instance, inform the texture of the sketch—reflecting the background of the writer and the subject rather than illustrating a
moral—and therefore many of the sketches succeed better than
some tales which try to illustrate a moral above all else. Here,
because Hogg remains himself, the result is natural and convincing. The shepherds' lives become known intimately because
Hogg not only observes but shares their knowledge.

### III    *Miscellaneous Prose*

With one exception, little need be said about Hogg's other nonfiction works. His inaccuracy makes the notes to the Burns edition
and the *Jacobite Relics* of little significance. The treatises "On
Sheep" and "The Statistics of Selkirkshire" contain much technical information, but could interest only an historian. Several
letters and occasional diatribes on politics and reviewers exist in
the magazines, but most are not worth reprinting or reading
because of their topicality or lack of literary merit.

The most extensive of these miscellaneous pieces is *A Series of
Lay Sermons on Good Principles and Good Breeding*, written in
the last years of his life. These good-humored, self-indulgent
homilies consist of advice from the aged man interspersed with
anecdotes and reflections about his own life. The strictures are
hardly profound, but they are not without their charm—Hogg
begins his preface by telling about the original source of the
maxims in order to prevent the awkwardness that will result when

"after the publication of this volume [he] shall be called to fill a chair of moral philosophy in some one of the cities of the United States, or Oxford at least."[13] The essays certainly reveal his prejudices as well as his beliefs. In educating children, he says, "Generosity would be the great virtue I should reward. Injustice, falsehood, cruelty, and ingratitude, would be almost the only crimes I should punish." He goes on to speak of his aversion to college education, a lifelong idea, since "I never saw any young man the better for it."[14] His reflections cover old age, young women (his age, he suggests, gives him the advantage of looking at feminine charms with a steadier and more discriminating eye), education, religion, and literary criticism. Despite his daughter's late Victorian plea that the forgotten *Sermons* are not unworthy of remembrance, it seems unlikely that their reappearance would add to his reputation. They remain the pleasant moralizings of a kindly and forthright old man, nothing more or less.

Far more important, both now and then, are Hogg's recollections of Scott. As the *Memoir* is among the first of his writings, the *Familiar Anecdotes of Sir Walter Scott* is among the last. At the conclusion of the section on Scott in the *Memoir*, Hogg had noted, "There are not above five people in the world who, I think, know Sir Walter better, or understand his character better than I do; and if I outlive him . . . I shall draw a mental portrait of him, the likeness of which to the original shall not be disputed" (*Mem*, 66). Scott's death in 1832 gave him the opportunity, although it was well known that Lockhart was preparing the official life (and jealously guarding his privilege). Hogg wrote his piece and sent it to America to avoid trouble; but in the absence of international copyright laws, the volume appeared in London as *The Domestic Manners and Private Life of Sir Walter Scott*.[15] The misleading title, which promises more than the book delivers, and Lockhart's objections[16] led to the book's poor reception and to Lockhart's damning comment on Hogg at the end of his *Life*. The devastating thirty-page anonymous review (written by William Maginn) in *Fraser's Magazine* begins by commenting that with his many autobiographies, Hogg "has made a perfect sty of our literature: and here we have him again. On the present occasion, however, we are entertained not merely with a grunt about himself, but he has impressed his hoofs on the memory of Sir Walter Scott." The review then details at length errors of fact, calls some writing "the work of a dull idiot," suggests that much is direct lie, and maintains that Hogg "was never on any footings of intimacy with the hero of his sketch,"[17] implying that Hogg has attempted to capitalize on the death of a mere acquaintance.

Yet the monograph was undoubtedly meant as a sincere tribute to one whom Hogg thought of as a great and kind friend and mentor. Given Hogg's faulty memory, his inclusion of so much of himself, even his occasional coarseness or lack of taste—characteristics of all his autobiographical writings—the pamphlet remains today not only the fullest record of the friendship between the two men, but also an important contemporary portrait of Scott—full of adulation but without undue sentimentality. The work presents the relationship between a feudal lord and one of his retainers, a valid and consistent image used by Hogg in a letter to Scott in 1821 beginning, "Like any other vassal whose situation with his chief is perfectly understood though never once mentioned, I always sit wisely still unless either called out by you to some great weapon show or when I find marauders and freebooters encroaching in my own privileges."[18] After repeating the Scott reminiscence from the *Memoir*, Hogg declares that "the only foible I ever could discover in the character of Sir Walter was a too strong leaning to the old aristocracy of the country. His devotion for titled rank was prodigious and in such an illustrious character altogether out of place" (*FA*, 95). He then describes Scott's ancestry, notes a "dinner in the feudal stile" which Hogg attended (98), indicates the concern over Hogg's having made Sir Walter Scott of Buccleuch the hero of *Three Perils of Man*, and reveals how Scott had not defended Hogg against a gamekeeper's lie to the Duke of Buccleuch.

The rest of the book deals with other aspects of Scott's character, adding little new but confirming the man's kindness and generosity and occasionally showing him to be human in his anger. "He was a most extraordinary being," Hogg writes, who "never was denied to any living neither lady or gentleman poor nor rich and he never seemed discomposed when intruded on but always good humoured and kind" (98-99). Hogg praises his friend for amusing and interesting conversation, poetry reading, attention especially to Mrs. Hogg and their children, discrimination about the characters of others, acceptance of both criticism and homage, abhorrence of low vices, and, above all, recognition of

Hogg and his works. In addition, Scott "was no great favorer of religion and seldom or never went to church. He was a complete and finished aristocrat and the prosperity of the state was his great concern which prosperity he deemed lost unless both example and precept flowed by regular gradation from the highest to the lowest" (128). In accordance with the conventional stratification of characters, Scott never uses the dialect, except in citing proverbs, though Hogg himself often speaks in broad Scots.

Structurally, the book is a horror. Though it begins with their first meeting and ends with their last and Scott's funeral, the intervening stories jump forward and back in time, sometimes linked by a common subject—such as Scott's discussions with Hogg concerning the latter's literary endeavors (although even here discussions from the 1820s precede those about *The Spy* of ten years earlier)—but most, especially toward the end, follow no particular pattern. As Hogg explains at the beginning, "I do not pretend to give a life of my illustrious and regretted friend. . . . The whole that I can presume to do is after an intimate acquaintance of thirty years to give a few simple and personal anecdotes which no man can give but myself" (95). This disjointed approach weakens the book, however, because the stories possess much of a sameness, involving just Hogg and Scott without much variety. Hogg saw only the literary adviser and the regarded, though hardly intimate friend, and although the book does chronicle these sides of his character, it cannot go beyond them. "I have depicted him exactly as he was as he always appeared to me," Hogg writes (132), and thereby admits the limitations.

Despite some of the Shepherd's typically extravagant opinions —for instance, that "the Whig ascendency in the British cabinet killed Sir Walter . . . broke his heart deranged his whole constitution and murdered him" (132)—and his characteristic fragmented approach, some picture of Scott does emerge and some interesting anecdotes are preserved. Yet, like most of Hogg's nonfiction, the book is essentially an autobiography; at one point Hogg even justifies a digression by referring to the "ruling passion of egotism [which] came across me" (97). Hogg's own works, for instance, form the subjects of Scott's most interesting literary pronouncements, and when Hogg comments on Scott's physique, marveling at the size of his arm muscles, he cannot refrain from noting that his own chest measured second only to Scott's. And in recounting an argument over a review, Hogg writes, "At that period the whole of the aristocracy and literature of our country were set against me and determined to keep me down nay to crush me to a nonentity; thanks be to God I have lived to see the sentiments of my countrymen completely changed" (105). Even at their last meeting, a moving account of Scott's physical dependence upon Hogg's "firm and sure" shoulder—an implied image of the vassal supporting his dying lord—the discussion turns upon Hogg, as Scott worries about "my welfare and success in life more than I had ever heard him do before and all mixed with sorrow for my worldly misfortunes." Scott later speaks of the Shepherd as "still the old man Hogg careless and improvident as ever," though in speaking of the proposed collection of tales, Scott comments about how Hogg has "written a great deal that might be made available . . . with proper attention" (133-34). If the *Familiar Anecdotes* adds little of substance to a portrait of Scott, it nevertheless enlarges and confirms earlier pictures of Hogg himself, and it would have been a shame had it not been written.

Taken as a whole, Hogg's nonfiction prose reveals his characteristic methods and his typical strengths and weaknesses. Basically anecdotal and autobiographical, these works achieve powerful and immediate effects through appeals to reality and truth; they show a fine eye for subjective description and the illustration of character through dialogue; and they draw heavily on the experiences and beliefs of Hogg's peasant background. On the negative side, they tend to be fragmented and without profundity of thought or theme; they show little variety of character, except in the person of Hogg himself. But that person—to recur as a narrator, persona, or character in the fiction—stands as the central achievement of the nonfiction. Not only did the Shepherd write his autobiography all his life, but he wrote autobiographically all his life, since his themes, subjects, and style all derive from his shepherd experiences and from the storytelling traditions passed on by his mother. As his public image grew, through his own works and through the *Noctes*, Hogg came more and more to use it in his writing: sketches and tales were signed "The Ettrick Shepherd" or simply dated from "Altrive Lake" and "Mount Benger," while poems dealt with explicit autobiographical material that the audience was expected to recognize. Finally, Hogg employed this image to create the illusion of fact.

The sixteenth-century Bard of Ettrick in *The Queen's Wake* embodies this public image. When he appears,

> The ladies smiled, the courtiers sneered:
> For such a simple air and mien
> Before a court had never been.
> A clown he was, bred in the wild, . . .
> The bard on Ettrick's mountain green
> In nature's bosom nursed had been,
> And oft had marked in forest lone
> Her beauties on her mountain throne; . . .
> Had viewed the Ettrick waving clear,
> Where shadowy flocks of purest snow
> Seemed grazing in a world below.
> Instead of Ocean's billowy pride,
> Where monsters play and navies ride,
> Oft had he viewed, as morning rose,
> The bosom of the lonely Lowes, . . .
> Instead of war's unhallowed form,
> His eye had seen the thunderstorm
> Descend within the mountain's brim,
> And shroud him in its chambers grim; . . .
> Instead of arms or golden crest,
> His harp with mimic flowers was dressed.
>
> (*Poems*, 20-21)

This self-portrait, which restates the pastoral background and limited opportunities mentioned throughout the *Memoir*, also suggests major concerns in other works: the natural settings, the substitution of pastoral realism for Romantic adventure, and the comic and mimic stances. And those works—the bulk of the poetry and prose—are the fruits of his autobiography.

CHAPTER 3

# *Conventional Poetry and Fiction*

S AMUEL Johnson observed that no man but a blockhead ever
wrote except for money, and there can be little doubt that
Hogg's literary aims were in great measure economic. He used his
literary earnings to rent and stock farms; he preferred the life of
the country, and was happiest there. He made little effort to
correct or revise his work, except for collected editions, and maintained throughout his life that he never reread anything that he
had written. Once he told the publisher James Ballantyne to send
the proofs of *Three Perils of Woman* to Scott for correction, but
Ballantyne replied, horrified, "He correct them for you! L--d help
you and him both! . . . He is the most careless and incorrect writer
that ever was born of a voluminous and popular writer and as for
sending a proof sheet to him we may as well keep it in the office.
He never heeds it" (*FA*, 131-32). Hogg's letters show that he sent
whatever was on hand to an annual without regard for the
magazine's audience.

Moreover, his works themselves often betray a simple, but
hardly admirable lack of concern for literary integrity. The poem
"Love Letter," for instance, lifts four stanzas from "Ah, Peggie,
since th'art gane away," and changes the tense from past to
present and the girl from Peggie to Maggy—and both appear in
the *Works*. Hogg acknowledges his often mechanical writing in
the final lines of "A Greek Pastoral": "Thus ends my yearly
offering bland,/The Laureate's Lay of the Fairy Land" (*Poems*,
294). As a seeker after patronage, Hogg also wrote many formal
and unmemorable poems to order, such as the hope that Buccleuch's banner, lifted at the "great foot-ball match" on Carter-
haugh, December 5, 1815, need never again be lifted on a sterner

field. The most ambitious of such poems was a masque, "The Royal Jubilee," which tells of the preparations of the fairies around Arthur's Seat for the Edinburgh visit of George IV. His poem on Shakespeare ("Spirit all limitless,/Where is thy dwelling-place?"), which reproduces the rhythm of his oft-praised "The Skylark" ("Bird of the wilderness,/Blithesome and cumberless"), was written upon his honorary membership in the Shakespearean Club.[1] Hogg's note to the poem "Wallace" does nothing to make the reader wish to go on: "This poem was reluctantly and hurriedly written in compliance with the solicitations of a friend who would not be gainsayed, to compete for a prize offered by a gentleman for the best poem on the subject. The prize was finally awarded to Mrs. Felicia Hemans; and, as far as the merits of mine went, very justly; hers being greatly superior both in elegance of thought and composition" (*Poems*, 377). Hogg fared as badly at the hands of editors as of publishers—even when he collected his own material —in the amount of poor work salvaged for collected editions.

The Shepherd was a gifted writer of "slick" fiction and poetry; he knew what would sell, and he produced it with skill and speed. And he could hardly be blamed, since the works he thought good received poor reviews, and those he deprecated or dashed off were popular. Moreover, his two most ambitious and original works in terms of theme, content, and technique—*Pilgrims of the Sun* and the *Confessions*—received almost no contemporary comment. Much of his later publication was revised from *The Spy*, and his works, taken in chronological order, show almost no sign of significant literary development. As he resolves, at various times in his letters and *Memoir*, first to give up writing drama, then poetry, it seems clear that he has more interest in the pecuniary side of art than in the art itself.

Nor does he concern himself with differences between prose and poetry. In *The Three Perils of Man*, during a storytelling contest, the poet tells of three Christian sisters whose faith proves a miraculous foil to the worshipers of Odin. The prose tale begins, "Once on a time, in that sweet northern land called Otholine, the heathen Hongar landed, and o'er-ran city and dale. The rampart and the flood in vain withstood his might. Even to the base of the unconquered Grampians did he wend with fire and sword."[2] Thirteen years later in *Fraser's Magazine* appears one of Hogg's last printed poems, "The Three Sisters," which begins:

Once on a time, in that sweet northern land
Called Otholine, the heathen Hongar landed,
And laid waste city, church, and fruitful dale—
The rampart and the flood in vain withstood him:
Even to the base of the unconquered Grampians
He bare with fire and sword.[3]

The poem continues for some twelve pages, with only occasional changes in wording and the addition of a few lines to accommodate poetic form. But, as in most of the Shepherd's poorer efforts, it takes more than line division to make poetry.

Hogg's ability to dash off publishable fiction, poetry, and reminiscence according to need—when a horse died, when new supplies were required—made for little change in technique, whatever the genre. Both tales and poems contain the same appeals to reality, the same autobiographical or fictional frame devices, and the same moral tone, along with parallel uses of dialogue to set scene or create character. In addition, similar subjects and themes, deriving from the folk traditions of his youth, appear in both genres. History, religion, love, morality, ghosts and fairies, and the pastoral life become trademarks as recognizable as "the Ettrick Shepherd" or "Altrive Lake."

The foregoing may seem to suggest that Hogg's lack of artistic seriousness should disqualify him from serious consideration. Yet even though many of his tales and poems are indeed repetitious or highly imitative of Burns and Scott (and, later, of himself), the epithet of "slick" or "hack" writer need not be pejorative. Even minor writers can produce a masterpiece, a work better, say, than the secondary works of an acknowledged master; formulas, too, have led to important works as well, as Shakespeare, Defoe, and many others have proved. Moreover, in Hogg's case especially, the fact remains that his formula pieces are usually of considerable quality. This chapter considers for the most part Hogg's minor works, formula pieces to be sure, but ones exemplifying his typical approaches—they represent Hogg at his average, not his worst, and the Shepherd's average was still good, judged both by contemporary standards and by today's.

The consideration of his conventional shorter works and his extended narratives, with as little distinction between prose and poetry as he himself made, makes clear exactly what the Shepherd was capable of. Moreover, since Hogg's best work—both those few pieces which have survived and those which have been unduly neglected—usually builds upon some of his basic techniques, it is useful to have in mind his typical writings before considering the ways in which he went beyond the formula to produce works of the highest quality. First, however, the Ettrick Shepherd's writings as his readers knew them.

## I  *Conventional and Moral Works*

Hogg began his literary career as a kind of minstrel producing songs for the shepherds and lasses of Ettrick. Other early poems included imitations of the Psalms or of the ballads and songs of first his mother, and later of Burns. In the first productions, lyrics, songs, and reflections of the pastoral life, it remains impossible to separate Hogg and Burns completely, even though their achievements differ considerably. During his own time, Hogg saw himself compared to the Ayrshire poet, as would be natural from their reputations as untutored "children of Nature." An article by Wilson on Scottish pastoral and agricultural poetry places Hogg second to Burns among such poets, though noting the "separate and distinct" characters of their works.[4]

Many of Hogg's pastoral lyrics sound familiar because they merely repeat the feelings and types of Burns's lyrics, without the latter's emotional involvement. The love poems express typical shepherdic sentiments about Maggy, or Peggy, or Mary, or even Jean, and the Scots dialect covers the absence of originality or even of strong emotion. As is often the case in Hogg's songs, the music is all important, while the words seem lifeless or border on cliché: "Oh, I had seen when fields were green, / An' birds sae blithe an' cheerie, O, / How swift the day would pass away / When I was wi' my dearie, O," but he'll "never taste o' pleasure mair, / Since I hae lost my Jeanie, O" (*Poems*, 270). Even the most famous of his lyrics, "When the Kye comes Hame," partakes of this familiarity, but the rhythms and the observations of nature rather than of people give it a distinction that raises it above the conventions:

> Come all ye jolly shepherds
> That whistle through the glen,

I'll tell ye of a secret
    That courtiers dinna ken:
What is the greatest bliss
    That the tongue o' man can name?
'Tis to woo a bonny lassie
    When the kye comes hame.
        When the kye comes hame,
        When the kye comes hame,
        'Tween the gloaming and the mirk,
        When the kye comes hame. . . .
When the blewart bears a pearl,
    And the daisy turns a pea,
And the bonnie lucken gowan
    Has fauldit up her e'e,
Then the laverock frae the blue lift
    Drops down, an' thinks nae shame
To woo his bonnie lassie
    When the kye comes hame.

                                        (*Poems,* 414)

Music is the heart of Hogg's lyrics, which show considerable variation in meter and form, yet never make such experimentation obtrusive, since the music—thanks to Hogg's tuneful youth and ear—always comes through. Rarely in the lyrics does the Shepherd falter in finding words to match his tunes or in making the tunes themselves clear even on a printed page. And rarely, too, does demonstrably bad poetry appear in the songs, whereas the longer poems show evidence of contrivance to eke out meter and stanzaic form. But in the dances, especially, and the war-songs, Hogg can be found at his delightful and exuberant best. "Dennis Delany," for example, exhibits both these traits:

In sweet Tipperary, the pride of the throng,
I have danced a good jig, and have sung a good song;
On the green, as I caper'd, I scarce bent the grass—
To a bottle a friend—and no foe to a lass.
At hurling, my fellow could never be found,
For whoever I jostled soon came to the ground;
And the girls all swore that they ne'er could meet any
Could tickle their fancy like Dennis Delany.
    With my whack about, see it out, Dennis my jewel,
    Och! why will you leave us? How can you be cruel?

> Paddy Whack may go trudge it, and Murtoch O'Blaney,
> We'll part with them all for dear Dennis Delany.
>
> (363-64)

Similar energetic rhythms occur in many of the comic songs, such as the chorus of "Love's like a Dizziness":

> O, love, love, love!
> Love is like a dizziness!
> It winna let a poor body
> Gang about his business!
>
> (274)

In "The Skylark" the rhythm suggests the bird soaring

> O'er fell and fountain sheen,
> O'er moor and mountain green,
> Over the red streamer that heralds the day,
> Over the cloudlet dim,
> Over the rainbow's rim,
> Musical cherub, soar, singing, away!
>
> (411)

And the "Witch's Chant" summons up the devil in regular beats:

> Over the dog-star, over the wain,
> Over the cloud, and the rainbow's mane,
> Over the mountain and over the sea,
> Haste—haste—haste to me!
>
> (396)

Variety and the consistently effective wedding of words to music are hallmarks of Hogg's lyrics. "The aim was song," as Robert Frost would say. Hogg's lyric successes derive from the best use of his own nature—love of music, generalized feelings of happiness, acceptance of what life offers—rather than from indulgence in profound emotion. Or, as Wilson's essay puts it, Hogg displays "kind and gentle affections [rather] than agitating passions,"[5] and when so doing is at his best.

Similar things occur in his reflective poems. When Hogg attempts to be profound, the result fails to convince, because he cannot handle abstract ideas, nor does he understand the range of humanity—here perhaps his greatest difference from Burns. An egotist of moderate and gentle passions, he could rarely create convincing characters or emotions contrary to his own. Hence he succeeds in the reflective poems when dealing with specifically autobiographical experiences—conventional farewells to his dog and his native soil; and the more moving, because more personal, "A Last Adieu," on the death of his mother; and "A Bard's Address to his Youngest Daughter." In the latter two poems Hogg uses conventional sentiments—"chill poverty" and grave flowers watered with "the tears of a son"—yet adds personal details to create the tribute. He tells of his mother's songs "of the field where the warrior bled; / The garland of blossom dishonoured too soon; / The elves of the greenwood, the ghosts of the dead, / And fairies that journeyed by light of the moon"— subjects which would, of course, become his own. So finally, the simple repeated statement, "I loved thee, my parent," gains force from the man, not the rhetoric. The final stanza emphasizes his love and sums up all that he owes her: "Adieu, my loved parent! the trial is past— / . . . / And long as the name of thy darling shall last / All due be the song and the honour to thee!" (388).

In like manner his poem on his daughter focuses on the details of Harriet's play, especially her mimicry of the animals. He begs for kisses in memory of the grandmother whom she had never seen, then of her grandfather and mother; meanwhile her name calls up thoughts of the Duchess of Buccleuch, Hogg's patroness. The father sees the child as a "sacred, blest memorial, / When I kiss thee, I kiss them all." In fact, "all I ever loved, or love, /In wondrous visions still I trace / While gazing on thy guiltless face" (397). Her mood changing, the child runs away, and the poet offers a conventional blessing at the end; but the recognition of his history in her innocence remains one of his better insights into the way adults look at their children. More conventional, the early "Address to his auld dog Hector" also gains much from the informal manner in which the poet talks to his faithful, but aging dog: "Come, my auld, towzy, trusty friend, / What gars ye look sae dung wi' wae?" Again, the focus is on observed detail, such as Hector's jealousy when the poet flirts with bonnie Meg, and on the dialect, a typical mixture of Scots and English,[6] a "flavor" which gives the situation a rustic air and allows for homely allu-

sions, as in "He who feeds the ravens young, / Lets naething pass
he disna see; / He'll sometime judge o' right an' wrang, / An'
aye provide for you an' me." The poet vows to maintain a home
for his faithful companion until death (98-99).

Two other of Hogg's best reflective poems, "The Monitors"
and "St. Mary of the Lowes," make similar uses of conventional
elements and personal experiences or observations. In the former,
Hogg begins with a fearful look at the harbingers of winter and
old age; but as he considers his situation—his fame as a poet, his
family—he can propose a toast and dismiss gloomy thoughts "like
morning dew, / An' we'll be blithe an' blither still." Earlier,
when comparing his fame with that of kings, he cries happily,
"The day's my own—I'm free / Of statemen's guile an' flattery's
train / . . . / The Shepherd is himself again!" The poem ends
conventionally with an aphorism about the ups and downs of the
world and his poetic determination (399), but the true feeling
comes from the personal details concerning the character of the
Shepherd already established in other works. Making use of other
traditions, "St. Mary of the Lowes" less successfully combines
two common reflective types, the churchyard meditation on past
death and glory and the expression of grief over a lost love. Here
Hogg uses a persona not of himself but of a fictional lover; but
the poem's power comes from the recital in the first half of the
illustrious though anonymous dead now buried in the churchyard,
the church itself now a ruin. Ancient Border chieftains, Covenanters, heroes, shepherds, rangers, and hunters, "Even Scotts,
and Kerrs, and Pringles, blended / In peaceful slumbers, rest
together, / Whose fathers there to death contended" (391-92).
The second half, however, refers vaguely to a dead girl and ends
with some conventional moralizing.

A final example of Hogg's typical techniques in reflective
poetry, the extremely effective "Storm of Thunder among
Mountains," works through first-person observation. An old man
tells an unbelieving traveler about an enormous thunderstorm and
reflects upon it. The picture of the storm, with the nuances of
atmospheric changes, stands among the clearest and most powerful of all Hogg's pure descriptions, rivaling the sketches of *The
Shepherd's Calendar*. The old man establishes his knowledge of
Nature's "features, all her hues, / And all her thousand voices,"
by describing the clouds,

> how they heave, and sail
> From cliff to cliff, roll down into the chasms,
> Then rise from the opposing steeps like spray—
> Is it not grand?—And think'st thou I not know
> Each boding hue, each movement, and each shade,
> Of that aerial ocean? What am I
> But as a wave of it?

Then, for over a hundred lines, the old man describes the storm in terms of sounds, scenes, and religious feeling. The morning sky goes black: "It was a hideous twilight. No bird sung; / The flocks forgot to feed, and stood and gazed, / Nor wist they what to dread." Then comes a rushing sound from somewhere, followed by louder and more furious sounds, and finally thunder, lightning "from the Almighty's hand," hail, rain, floods;

> the rending peal
> Made the rocks chatter, rolled from hill to hill,
> And boomed along the sky. . . .
> Then tell not me of nature's operations;
> That was no produce of her onward work,
> But a dire judgment and a grievous one,
> As all the land hath found. My Bible calls
> Thunder the voice of the Eternal God.

After a sinful thought that "the fiends / Had met in conclave in that hollow cloud" and that the Almighty had been angered at them,

> the glorious sun looked from on high,
> Through golden windows opening in the cloud,
> In mild and glowing majesty, it was
> Like a glad glimpse of heaven to me, who had
> Sat in the shadow of infernal gloom
> Amid its horror, uproar, and turmoil;
> I could not choose but hail the God of Day,
> And King of Glory on his triumph won.
>
>                                          (381-83)

The reality derives from both character and description, and the religious moral—nature as the vocabulary of the all-powerful Creator—is wholly integrated with both; the detailed observation gives credibility to the old man, and his beliefs seem the firmer and more convincing for the way he sees things. The poem could be a study for Edgar Allan Poe's "Descent into the Maëlstrom," which employs many similar devices in no more sophisticated a way.

This moral tone, successfully integrated here and common throughout the writings, serves as the sole impetus of most of Hogg's undistinguished tales and poems which subordinate everything to the effort to teach their lesson. Such exempla recur throughout Hogg's literary career, as in the ballad "Maria, A Highland Legend," in which the beautiful Maria dies after having been seduced and abandoned by the Lord of the Mountain; afterwards, however, her spirit haunts him, and he finally drowns on a clear day; his name and power die out, a proof of "Heaven's just vengeance" (*Spy*, No. 17). "Maria's Tale," originally "The Country Girl" in *The Spy*, tells of the narrator's seduction and her current feelings against all men. The story takes the form of a letter to The Spy, always represented as "anxious to instruct and to reform," which advises the young and thoughtless "never to part with their virtue; for it is only by preserving that inviolate that they can secure love and esteem from the other sex, respect from their own, the approbation of their own hearts, or the love of their Creator" (*Spy*, No. 22).

Immoral actions receive swift punishment along with the author's lectures. In "The Hunter of Comar," the main character kills two roes who turn into dying babies, then into serpents; he wakes to find all a terrifyingly real nightmare, and he thanks God for this lesson about his own guilt and cruelty to animals.[7] The villain of "Welldean Hall" dies "unlamented, the victim of youthful folly and unrestrained libertinism" (*Tales*, 185). Sometimes Hogg gets completely carried away with his summary of purpose, as at the end of "Nancy Chisholm," when he writes, "This is a true story, and it contains not one moral, but many, as every true portraiture of human life must do. It shows us the danger of youthful imprudence, of jealousy, and of unruly passions; but, above all, it shows that without a due sense of religion there can be no true and disinterested love" (*Tales*, 418). Such warnings, drawing on Hogg's belief in Providential justice, serve as the moral basis for his conventional tales and poems.

As implied above, Hogg directs most of his moralizing at

women, both his major subject and his audience. With his own interest in the ballads, many of which also turn on love and betrayal for their plots, it seems only natural that most of Hogg's moral tales deal with seduction. Again, the handling is conventional: in happy endings the woman marries her lover and becomes an honest woman, and in tragic stories she delivers a stillborn baby, or dies herself, or both. The wicked and unprincipled, or youthful and misguided, lovers also come to gruesome ends (unless, of course, they marry), usually having been pursued by real, imagined, or disguised phantoms of the betrayed girl. Hogg's seduction tales become so much a stock-in-trade that, like the heroines of sentimental and Gothic novels, it becomes impossible to distinguish among the assorted Marias, Ellens, or Elizabeths, or, indeed, among the tales themselves. In advertising "Maria's Tale," Hogg writes, "M.M. shall have a place. Seduction is rather a hackneyed and precarious subject, but the simplicity of her narrative commands respect" (*Spy*, No. 17). The poem "Moralitas" stands as lecture without narrative, as Hogg admonishes, "She that giveth heart away / For the homage of a day, / . . . / Gains the curse that leaves her never; / Gains the pang that lasts for ever" (*Poems*, 387). Other works, however, detail the resulting misfortunes, as in "The Gloamin'," where the heroine, forced to leave home, returns to find "Her aged parents' hearts were broke"; her "fondest earthly hope was gone. . . . / Her heart abused, her love misused, / Her parents drooping to the tomb, / Weeping, she fled to desert bed, / To perish in its ample dome" (*Poems*, 266). In so many of Hogg's traditional pieces, only the occasionally varied supernatural elements raise them above formula.

On the other side of the seduction motif, however, Hogg shows the divine power against which no evil can prevail. In "The Spirit of the Glen," a ballad done almost entirely in dialogue, Marjory dismisses the warnings about a dreadful spirit with the words, "Have you not heard, Sir Dominie, / That face of virgin bears a charm, / And neither ghaist, nor man, nor beast, / Have any power to do her harm?" The churchman answers that "virgin beauty is on earth / The brightest type we have of heaven," though he warns her of presuming upon her virtue. Marjory goes off to meet her lover and first encounters a demon in the form of a beautiful youth, but her faith saves her. Then the Spirit of the

Glen appears and shows her her lover about to kill his current paramour before meeting his new one. Having learned her lesson, Marjory is returned to the Dominie's house, where he marries her. And the ballad ends, "Now, maidens dear, in greenwood shaw, / Ere you make trysts with flattering men, / Think of the sights poor Marjory saw, / And the Great Spirit of the Glen" (*Poems*, 329-32). A comic variation of the motif occurs in "O, Jeanie, there's naething to fear ye!" when the lover uses the belief as an argument for arranging a meeting. Come in the evening, he pleads,

> Far, far will the bogle an' brownie be,
>     Beauty an' truth they darena come near it;
> Kind love is the tie of our unity,
>     A' maun love it, an' a' maun revere it. . . .
> Oh, Jeanie, there's naething to fear ye!
>
> (*Poems*, 413)

Nothing except, perhaps, the lover himself. Hogg's moral outlook, conventional in itself and usually expressed conventionally, permeates his works, sometimes effectively, often blatantly, but always like the man himself—honest and simple, firm and unshakable.

## II  *Extended Narratives*

If Burns was Hogg's first literary model, Scott soon became the man most worthy of imitation. Not, of course, that Hogg was unique in following Scott, since the success of *The Lay of the Last Minstrel* (1805), *Marmion* (1808), and *The Lady of the Lake* (1810) brought forth a host of imitations, and long narrative poems became fashionable. When Scott's poetic impulse failed, and Byron's romances became popular, the Wizard of the North turned to prose with the enormously successful Waverley novels beginning in 1814. Hogg notes in the *Familiar Anecdotes*, "As long as Sir Walter Scott wrote poetry there was neither man nor woman ever thought of either reading or writing any thing but poetry. But the instant that he gave over writing poetry there was neither man nor woman ever read it more! All turned to tale and novels which I among others was reluctantly obliged to do. Yes I was obliged from the tide the irresistible current that followed him to forego the talent which God had given me at my birth and enter into a new sphere with which I had no acquaintance" (*FA*, 124).

Hogg wrote six extended narratives, three poems and three novels, which include the best and the worst of his writing. Two of the poems clearly imitate Scott, but one shows considerable originality of both theme and method; two of the novels also resemble popular types, the Waverley books on the one hand and domestic novels of manners on the other, but the *Confessions* also uses conventional elements in an original manner. These works show how Hogg, in trying to deal with a range far beyond his normal field of anecdote and personal experience, generally fails to maintain even his own interest and drifts off into subplots or other directions obviously not originally intended. The two successful books—*Pilgrims of the Sun* and the *Confessions*—have a unity and interest which the others lack; they also avoid Hogg's typical flaws by maintaining a restricted focus on the story. The other pieces, however, exhibit the characteristic result of Hogg's attempts at sustained poetry and prose: flashes of brilliance mixed with some of the poorest and most confused of his writing.

All the Shepherd's efforts prior to 1815 had been in the anecdotal style. Even the novelette-length tales of *The Spy* had been episodic, whereas *The Queen's Wake* merely assembled a series of ballads and short narratives under the frame of the minstrel contest. When he turned to longer forms, he experienced his main difficulty in keeping the plot consistent and comprehensible. *Mador of the Moor* is perhaps the most successful in terms of story, though most forgettable in terms of everything else. The simplicity of the tale, even its similarity to *Lady of the Lake*, no doubt helped the author keep it in hand. It follows the hero of the title, a wandering minstrel, who seduces a beautiful Highland girl, Ila Moore, but then disappears. She and her baby travel to Stirling to find the minstrel, supposedly attached to the royal court, and the Abbot of Dunfermline presents her case. The king promises justice, and then reveals himself as Mador traveling in disguise among his subjects. He marries Ila and makes her Queen of Scotland—virtue, justice, and beauty triumph. It is, quite simply, Hogg's conventional seduction tale, spiced with the motif of the disguised king. Little action occurs, and the Spenserian stanza, rarely used by Hogg, seems confining and unnatural, especially in the long speeches which make his stock characters even less believable.

The two long novels contain far more intricate plots, both of which get out of hand. *The Three Perils of Man* begins in an historical fashion, after the Waverley novels, by recounting the siege of Roxburgh Castle undertaken by James Douglas to win the hand of the Lady Margaret; since the castle was originally captured by the English Lord Musgrave to win Lady Jane Howard, Hogg sets up a nice parallel to explore the nature of chivalry. The two heroines play important roles in the opening pages, along with Sir Ringan Redhough, a powerful Border baron. The latter then determines to send to the famous warlock, Michael Scott, to learn the outcome of the siege, and the central portion of the novel follows the exploits of this party, led by the yeoman Charlie (Scott) Yardbire and including a poet, a philosophic lord, a friar, a glutton, and a beautiful girl. The friar, who proves to be Roger Bacon, contends with the wizard, as the whole group encounters a series of fantastic and episodic adventures; half a volume consists of interpolated stories told to while away their time when imprisoned in the warlock's castle. Finally, the scene shifts back to Roxburgh for the lifting of the siege amid much bloodshed, and the heroes and heroines pair off in mechanical fashion. Hogg later followed Scott's advice to cut the supernatural sequences, keeping only the historical and realistic passages, so that the novel appeared in the *Works* as a novelette, "The Siege of Roxburgh."

The next year, Hogg turned from history to contemporary manners for the *Three Perils of Woman*. Here, although the major characters stay at the center of their stories, Hogg never quite decides what kind of novel he is writing. This standard "three-decker" in fact consists of two long tales. The first begins as a domestic tragedy—a love triangle involving Gatty Bell, her cousin Cherry Elliot, and her lover M'Ion of Boroland—which culminates in the death by heartbreak of Cherry, but then shifts to a fine horror tale in which Gatty, unhinged by her cousin's death, remains in a catatonic state for three years before waking on the anniversary of her original fit to take up her life as if nothing had happened. A subplot concerning Gatty's father and his confusion in the big city adds little besides some comedy to the main tale and, indeed, often seems out of place. The novel's other story, comprising the third volume, breaks into two distinct and almost unrelated parts, the first a comic tale of Sally Niven, who juggles lovers of all ages and degrees through clever tricks and lies, and the second a tragic tale of Culloden in which the two main characters mature and develop to an extent unusual in Hogg's work. This last part stands among the Shepherd's most effective historical narratives—lucid and fast-paced, with some moving, understated pictures of the days following the massacre.

*Queen Hynde* marks a return to the historical, epic romance of the earlier years, and though poetically weak nevertheless boasts a fairly clear, if conventional, plot, along with two spirited heroines. It does show, however, a facility with most of the clichés of the verse romance, by that time outdated. The story concerns a beautiful young Scottish queen whose realm is attacked by the Norwegian, Eric, seeking both the queen and the country. Her confessor, St. Columba, learns from her father's ghost about a cousin, the rightful heir, who has been raised in Ireland; Columba sails there, but fails to receive aid from the king, though on his return a dark, wild young Irishman saves the boat in a storm. After a series of battles, culminating in a superb duel between Eric and the young stranger—the cousin, Prince Eiden, of course— Scotland is saved and the heathens driven off. The romantic ending, however, is slightly undercut by the invaders' final attempt to save themselves: the successful sacrifice of nine virgins, selected from a hundred hostages with "Those that remain'd by lot . . . shared/Amongst the soldiers of the guard" (*Poems*, 260). A parallel love story involving the flirtatious Wene, one of Hynde's ladies-in-waiting, and Prince Haco, Eric's successor, gains most interest due to the girl's sprightly character; here Hogg attempts to present the personal on one level, the historical on another. In any event, if *Mador*, a decade earlier, lacked action, *Queen Hynde* contains more than enough for both.

In addition to the overriding difficulties in maintaining coherence of plot in the long works, Hogg demonstrates as well some of his worst writing. Such lapses can perhaps be overlooked more easily in the prose tales, where much of the incoherence derives from interpolated stories or changes of direction which, considered as anecdotes or entities complete in themselves, often retain considerable interest; as part of the novels, however, they do not fit the main tone or theme.[8] In the poetry, and especially in *Queen Hynde*, the verse seems repetitive, imprecise, and tired.

Expletives increase and the tone becomes inconsistent; the line lengths shift for no apparent reason, and the inverted word order continually astonishes with its ineptitude. King Colmar of Ireland, for instance, awaits the coming of Columba, vowing in advance not to give aid, for, he explains,

> Small good to Erin have they done;
> For though this father bears a name
> Of sanctitude and reverend fame
> I've always found that horde a pest,
> An ulcer, and a hornet's nest.
> Their cause is lost ere they appear;
> I'm quite in mood their suit to hear.

Columba's plea combines weak rhetoric with bad poetry: "Oh, King of Erin, hear me speak,/And see the tears on my wan cheek,/ I seek the prince, his own to gain;/In Albyn his the right to reign" (*Poems*, 212). Later, the impetuous Haco breaks the truce in a skirmish with the Scots and implores his troops in elevated language not to mention the incident; when Haco meets his uncle, however, he withholds his "blabbing tongue." Hogg seems so fond of the word that a few lines later the Scots hero tells what he would do if Eric's priest discloses the affair: "I'd let him blood, and make his bed/Full fifty feet below my tread,/Rather than he should blab disgrace/On great M'Ola's royal race" (222). In the encounter between three heroes from each side, Donald's "bronzied" cheek seems less a description than a quick means of filling the line (226). Despite some fine moments, such as in the battle scenes where Hogg has action that he can attend to or in occasional lines like that describing a club which "swither'd through the air" (243), *Hynde* remains for the most part a poem which could have remained unfinished without serious loss.

The long works also include the moral concerns discussed earlier, or at least purport to deal with them. The frame story of *Hynde*, developed at the end of each of the poem's six parts, shows the poet telling his story to the Maid of Dunedin; he begins by wishing to entertain her, but then in Part Second starts to lecture on "this jointered age . . ./This age of bond and bank-ruptcy—/With all its sordid thirst of gold," and on how his heroic lay is in contrast to this world. Women again become his true sub-ject, as he admits singing "Of maiden's guilt and failings too;/

And all in love to paint to thee/The charms of perfect purity"
(*Poems*, 204). Likewise, *The Three Perils of Woman* focuses on
specific moral aspects, as the subtitle, "Love, Leasing, and
Jealousy," suggests. Built in a complex but inconsistent series of
circles (supposed to recall Dante), the first story illustrates "that,
YOUTHFUL LOVE IS THE FIRST AND GREATEST PERIL
OF WOMAN,"[9] whereas the second tale's two parts inveigh
against lying and jealousy. But, as so often happens in Hogg's
long works, he loses sight of his purpose and (often happily) gets
carried away by the story. Hence, the jealousy which the heroine
refuses to reveal to her husband when she believes him in love
with another is only mentioned once in mid-tale and never at the
end. Sally's lying nature, moreover, is one of the charming parts
of her character and does as much to get her out of trouble as to
get her in. Also, the follies of youthful love exhibited by the
heroines of the first story—the sober-minded Gatty and the
flirtatious Cherry—result not really from an inherent weakness of
love, but from extreme and unnatural early training: Gatty has
been taught "the leading duty of self-denial" (*3PW*, I, 5), and
Cherry's death from melancholia and a broken heart results from
her romantic renunciation of M'Ion, so that the story becomes an
often fascinating study of emotional extremism.

Such fascination suggests that the extended narratives, even the
poorer ones, do not lack interest. Indeed, the interpolated stories
and supernatural accounts of *Three Perils of Man* and the
extended battle sequences of *Queen Hynde* show Hogg's gift for
telling exciting and wondrous stories. The duel of wizardry with
Michael Scott, which explains the forming of the Eildon Hills,
and the individual contests of skill and strength in *Hynde* illustrate his power of recreating supernatural and physical action.
And the descriptions of Highland scenery in *Mador* and of the
Culloden fields in *Three Perils of Woman* reveal his methods of
presenting direct observation at their best. The Spenserian stanzas
of *Mador*, when not containing the wretched dialogue of the weak
characters, fulfill Hogg's expectations in selecting it to depict the
"majesty and grandeur" of "mountains, cataracts, and storms"
(*Mem*, 32). Like *Lady of the Lake*, *Mador* begins with a hunt,
with the king's progress followed through various colors of the
sunrise, changing clouds on the hills, and echoing sounds of the
hunt in the valleys. Later, a thunderstorm comes down in much

the same way as in "Storm of Thunder among Mountains," with concentration on the sound and the superstitious effect of the storm on the heroine and an old palmer who lie awake all night, fearing that fiends will take the unblessed child in their charge. Unfortunately, such descriptions give way to cliché and inflated rhetoric as Mador and Ila gain prominence.

Hogg's rather sketchy battlefield descriptions in *Three Perils of Woman* prove, however, the effectiveness of just a few horrific details. He disingenuously prefaces his scene with an apology: "I am now compelled, both from want of room, and want of inclination to the task, to desist from the description of some dreadful scenes that followed the events above narrated. But, as they are the disgrace of the British annals, it is perhaps as well that I am obliged to pass over them, although it makes a breach in a tale that has always been one of the deepest interest to me" (*3PW*, III, 44-45). Then Hogg spends a hundred pages in isolated details and anecdotes of Culloden, including glimpses of atrocities, like the half-roasted bodies of a mother and her two sons, of the burials of bodies and parts of bodies, and of the comic character Davie Duff, now become "earther-general" for the Duke of Cumberland, his job being to cut ears off the corpses as proof of the number of Highland dead. The fiction corroborates the disaster as the heroine's husband, through a series of misunderstandings, shoots Peter Gow, Sally's first love, and is stabbed by him in return; both men are finally brutally murdered by English troops, and Sally, going mad, dies on her husband's grave. "Is there human sorrow on record like this that winded up the devastation of the Highlands?" Hogg concludes. "Just God! was it as the old Celtic bard and seer had predicted? Was it a retribution from thy omnipotent hand for the guiltless blood shed in the south of Scotland by the House of Stuart and their Highland host?" (*3PW*, III, 371). These final pictures, grimly effective and moving, are a long way, however, from the avowed purpose of delineating jealousy as a peril of womankind. The story has gone far beyond the original moral intent and novel of manners to present scenes of universal significance.

The long narratives also afford Hogg scope in dealing with character and theme that he has elsewhere had little opportunity to develop. Although the characters often seem the stock figures of nineteenth-century romance, as defined by Scott especially, many take on a fullness impossible in Hogg's shorter pieces where everything is made subordinate to story. This new range is obvious in the *Confessions*, where one character, Robert Wringhim, stands at the center of the book; others of the long works with their complex plots provide differentiation between similar characters. In *Three Perils of Man*, for example, the traits of Sir Ringan, James Douglas, and Charlie Yardbire all receive considerable attention. The first two are noblemen, and their portraits set up the chivalric/realistic tension that forms one of the novel's main themes. Douglas acts always by the romantic forms of chivalry: he vows to end the siege to win his lady and to defend Scottish honor; he honors truces, though executing spies according to the rules of war. As he says to Lord Musgrave at a meeting under truce, "And how wide is the difference between the prizes for which we contend? I for my love, my honour, and the very existence of my house and name; and you for you know not what,—the miserable pride of opposition. Take your measures, my lord, I will not be mocked" (*3PM*, 68).

Sir Ringan, on the other hand, is humanized not only by his more realistic outlook, but by his family as well. His immediate response upon hearing that Douglas has taken up Lady Margaret's challenge to free Roxburgh and win her, is refusal: "What, man, are a' my brave lads to lie in bloody claes that the Douglas may lie i' snaw-white sheets wi' a bonny bedfellow?" (*3PM*, 5). But Sir Ringan is also cursed with a wife who dislikes both his drinking companions and his slurs on chivalry. She tells him,

"for all your bravery, candour, and kindness, you are a mere novice in the affairs of life, and know less of men and of things than ever knight did."

"It is a great fault in women," said the knight, making his observation general, "that they will aye be meddling wi' things they ken nought about. They think they ken every thing, an' wad gar ane trow that they can see an inch into a fir deal.—Gude help them! It is just as unfeasible to hear a lady discussing the merits of warriors an' yeomen, as it wad be to see me sitting nursing a wench-bairn."

"Foh, what an uncourtly term!" said the lady; "What would King Robert think if he heard you speaking in that uncouth stile?"

"I speak muckle better than him, wi' his short clippit Highland tongue," said the chief. (*3PM*, 10-11)

The leader of Sir Ringan's prudent expedition, Charlie Yardbire, combines Douglas's martial ability with Sir Ringan's realistic outlook, and becomes the most appealing of all the heroes. Charlie rescues beautiful women and performs individual deeds of valor in battle with a level-headed innocence and determination, mixed with charm, that gives him an aura somewhat removed from that of traditional romantic heroes. After he and Sir Ringan lead a band of soldiers into Roxburgh to break the siege, Charlie, now a knight, wins the English Lady Jane for his wife. When he first meets her, however, taking her as prisoner to Douglas, he rejects her bribes with simple country wisdom: "What does it signify for a man to hae mair gear than he can count?" And later, "Your offer's ower muckle, an' that makes me dread there's something at the bottom o't that I dinna comprehend. Gude faith, an [Sir Ringan] war to suffer danger or disgrace for my greed o' siller, it wad be a bonny story," and he urges his horse to "get on, I say, an' dinna gie me time to hear another word or think about this business again" (*3PM*, 44). When later told that the prisoner was actually "the greatest beauty, and the greatest heiress in England," and asked what he would have done had he known, Charlie answers, "Gude faith, it was as weel I didna ken" (*3PM*, 45).

With these few exceptions, however, Hogg's heroes tend to be traditionally romantic, that is, brave, handsome, young, strong, sometimes mysterious, and usually insipid. The heroes of *Queen Hynde* have only different physical attributes to distinguish them from one another. Of the hero of *Mador*, even less can be said, for whether disguised as a minstrel or arrayed in kingly splendor, he fails to exhibit anything other than stock heroic traits. The heroines, on the other hand, often break the traditional patterns. In fact, Hogg's treatments of women, both conventional and unconventional, form perhaps his most consistent thematic interest, as he tells his listener in *Queen Hynde*:

> I've sung of wake and roundelay,
> In beauteous Mary's early day;
> Of charms that could all hearts command;
> Of maiden borne to fairy land;
> Of worlds of love and virgins bright;
> Of pilgrims to the land of light.
> And I have sung to those who know

> Of maiden's guilt and failings too;
> And all in love to paint to thee
> The charms of perfect purity.
>  Now I've call'd forth a patriot queen
> Of generous soul and courtly mien;
> And I've upraised a wayward elf
> With faults and foibles like thyself;
> And these as women thou shalt see,
> More as they are than they should be.
>                                            (*Poems*, 204)

Though most of Hogg's women are victims—of men's lusts or their own failings or both—or chivalric objects and rewards, many of them nevertheless display a strength of character and action, and a determination and sense of reality unusual for the romantic heroine. The situations of victim or mourner derive from the ballads, but those active heroines who know their own minds and their own desires certainly come from Hogg's realistic and generally antiromantic outlook.

As he notes in the summary, the two heroines in *Hynde* differ in the same ways as the heroes of his prose romance: Hynde, regal and courtly, tries to do the best for her country and people by offering herself as a hostage and, if need be, as a wife; her companion, however, deemed "wicked Wene," a lively, mischievous wench, attempts to seduce all men in sight for her own pleasure. Hogg describes her as "A lovely thing, of slender make,/Who mischief wrought for mischief's sake;/And never was her heart so pleased/As when a man she vex'd or teased" (*Poems*, 192). In her first appearance she flirts with the venerable Saint Oran, and she succeeds to such an extent that he undertakes severe physical penance despite his age. She becomes in the course of the poem a tongue-in-cheek object lesson for the poem's putative listener on the follies of waywardness and flirtation; actually, however, she becomes the true heroine by impersonating Hynde and taking her place as hostage in the enemy camp. At the end she marries Prince Haco and becomes Queen of Scandinavia, a reward for her bravery. Throughout the poem, her liveliness provides the few touches of humanity, as in her defense of the condemned virgins, which appeals to sense on the one hand and reputation on the other; she tells Eric,

> If you would please
> Great Odin, and his wrath appease,
> Preserve us lovely, living things,
> An offering to your King of kings.
> For, should you dare suppose that he,
> A god, so brutalized could be,
> As in dead virgin to delight
> More than in living beauty bright,
> You shall stand beacons of his scorn,
> And rue the time that you were born!
>   But what is more . . .
> Think of a sovereign's sacred blood;
> And for a word in churlish mood
> Dare not to break through law divine,
> And bring a curse on all your line.
>
> (235-36)

Earlier, in offering to take Hynde's place, Wene flaunts her powers and her delightful egotism in responding to Hynde's gift of a dowry:

> Preserve your interest for yourself,
> My generous queen; for you may need
> That and some more, in marriage speed.
> For me, henceforth I'll use mankind
> As I would do the passing wind—
> To breathe upon, and bid it fly
> Away from great important I!
> Or to supply this ardent breast
> With cooling laughter and with jest.
>
> (230)

The heroines of *Three Perils of Woman* show the same contrast, but with even greater distinction between their characters because Hogg provides more of their backgrounds and more scenes of their interaction with others. In the main story, the two girls resemble Hynde and Wene. Gatty, proper, protected, devout, and introspective, keeps her emotions to herself, as does Hynde, and relies on outward forms as protection against the free reign of her feelings. She prays at the beginning of the story "that she might be preserved from all sin and temptation, and never left to follow the dictates of her own corrupt heart" (*3PW*, I, 6).

Ignoring her country father's advice to "learn to manage your head, your hands, your feet, and your heart" and not to affect the "snappy English pronunciation" over the Scots tongue (I, 25, 28), Gatty goes to Edinburgh distrustful of her own emotions and heeding instead the warnings of her nurse against "youthful love." She comes to realize how much misconception, grief, and jealousy result from the modern fashion of concealing one's true sentiments, but she continues to do so, avoiding her lover, M'Ion, refusing his advances, denying the love she feels for him to her friends. These denials finally bring about the catastrophe when Cherry takes them at face value and inveigles from M'Ion a proposal. Though Cherry finally releases him from his promise, it is at the cost of her own life and the near death of Gatty.

Cherry, like "wicked Wene," represents the opposite side of the female character as well as the opposite side of repressed emotions. She flirts and teases openly and irrationally; she artfully manipulates M'Ion. Finally, though, convinced that M'Ion and Gatty love one another, she heroically renounces him, asking only for a yellow gown, the color of forsaken maidens. As Gatty's bridesmaid, however, she forgets to take the bride's glove and unconsciously puts her own hand in M'Ion's at the minister's request. Afterwards, she becomes ill, asks M'Ion for the one kiss he had promised, and dies. Says a friend, after the renunciation, "The little elf is absolutely a heroine. There is something in the constitution of her mind capable of being raised to a height that would render her one of the first order of mortal beings" (II, 42). But though her death is melodramatic, it results in a realistic sequel: Gatty's morbid despair eventually sends her into a catatonic shock. The comedy of manners has become tragedy and horror, and if the tone shifts, the theme is clear: people must avoid extremes of emotion and follow the dictates of common sense. Here is Hogg's principal gospel of moderation preached through people rather than puppets. "We must . . . be content still," the narrator comments, "to take human life as it is, with all its loveliness, folly, and incongruity" (II, 243).

The two heroines in *The Three Perils of Man* are also clearly distinguished, and though they conform more to romantic ideals, they have learned to use that position realistically to their own advantage. Neither contents herself with merely sitting back and being contended for. Lady Margaret, who issued the original challenge to the Scots barons, immediately disguises herself as a man and plunges into the conflict, hoping to spy out some advantages for her side. Shortly thereafter she meets Lady Jane, disguised as a prince, who has come to Scotland to observe the contest for *her* hand. Scott told Hogg that "the meeting of the two princesses at Castle-Weiry is excellent. I have not seen any modern thing more truly dramatic" (*FA*, 101). Margaret, disguised as Prince Alexander Stuart en route to a noble English family, is forward, charming, witty and slightly bawdy; Jane, in the role of Jasper Tudor traveling to determine the suitability of the Scottish princess, Margaret, as a wife, first appears with a similar manner, but soon retreats to a feminine shyness. Their conversation starts on Margaret's reputation, much to her discomfort, so she turns the discussion to Jane, rumored to be "a shrew and a coquette, a wicked minx, that is intemperate in all her passions." Thereupon "Tudor" blushes and answers, "It is a manifest falsehood, I never knew a young lady so moderate and chastened in every passion of the female heart. Her most private thoughts are pure as purity itself" (*3PM*, 28-29). That purity leads to her discovery, however, for when Tudor refuses to sleep with the men, and when the two daughters of the house, "who visibly wanted a romp with the young blooming chief," try to undress him, Margaret realizes the truth and, after some bawdy teasing, arranges for Jane's capture and removal to Douglas's camp.

Margaret's adventures don't stop there, for she soon enters Roxburgh Castle itself, disguised as a page, but is captured, her identity undiscovered. When Douglas hangs Musgrave's brother, the Englishman retaliates by executing all his Scots captives, including the "gaudy page," who is unceremoniously carried "to the battlement of the western tower, from whence, sans farther ceremony, he was suspended from a beam's end" (*3PM*, 87). Without doubt, the hanging of his heroine one-sixth of the way through the book is one of Hogg's finest surprises. Even when she reappears as a ghost to direct Douglas's acts, the reader can never quite be sure about the reality of her death; since other supernatural events do occur, and since major figures like Musgrave's brother and even Musgrave himself die before the denouement, the "death" of Margaret can be seen as another impingement of reality on the chivalric background. If the hurried account of her survival seems somewhat disappointing—like most such explana-

tions in Hogg and others—the actual effect of her supposed
execution remains impressive. It also reinforces Hogg's antiromantic stance; like the actual sacrifice of the virgins in *Queen
Hynde*, or the death of Cherry and the madness of Gatty, the
gruesome reality undercuts the sentimentality of the romantic
form in which he writes.

In fact these intrusions of reality become a recurrent motif in
this book, as in other tales and poems. What happens is not that
war, women, and witchcraft become the three perils of man, but
that chivalric excess stands as the real threat because it dehuman-
izes, besides causing realistic death. Despite the surface romance,
Hogg constantly undercuts what chivalry has done to its adherents.
Douglas speaks "the extravagant bombast peculiar to that age. He
called her his guardian angel, his altar of incense, and the saint of
his devotion, the buckler of his arm, the sword in his hand, and
the jewel of his heart. 'Do you think, Colin,' added he, 'that ever
there was a maiden born like this royal lady of my love?' " And
Colin, the disguised Margaret, answers, "She is well formed. And
yet she is but so so" (*3PM*, 70). Even the heroines, usually more
clever than the men, fall victim to the system. Margaret, in
deciding what to do about the disguised Lady Jane, begins to
ponder, "and well she knew that, whichever side succeeded,
according to the romantic ideas of that age, the charms of the
lady would have all the honour, while she whose hero lost would
be degraded,—considerations which no woman laying claim to
superior and all-powerful charms could withstand" (*3PM*, 36). At
the end Margaret feels terribly slighted, for Musgrave has killed
himself to uphold his honor, but Margaret has only become Lady
Douglas; she criticizes her husband to her friend, "But he was too
selfish, and would not die for me. Base, cruel knight! No, he
*would not* die for me; even though I got him to believe that I was
put to death, and my ghost haunting him, yet he *would not* kill
himself. What a value those monstrous men set upon their lives!
Musgrave died. Lady Jane has conquered, and I am *married*! I
wish I were dead, Kirmichael!" (*3PM*, 434). For all her liveliness
and quick wit, Margaret remains as much a product of unhappy
teaching as Gatty Bell.

This use of realism becomes clearest in the final volume of
*Three Perils of Woman* when Culloden leads to the deaths of all
three main characters. Two of them, Peter Gow and Sally, stand

among Hogg's best characterizations. Peter, the blacksmith's son in love with the minister's housekeeper, changes from a poacher involved in an almost comic murder to a hero who leads a group of eleven old men in defense of Prince Charlie and utterly routs the Earl of Loudon. After both Peter and Sally are treated as heroes, each feels that marriage with the other would be beneath him, so Peter goes home and marries a country maid, and Sally a Highland gentleman. When they meet again after Culloden, they become deep friends, clearly having matured and repented the hastiness of their earlier years, though Sally remains faithful to her spouse. Quick-witted as Wene and Margaret—her stories and actions save both Peter and the minister from reprisals, while she fends them off as suitors—Sally remains totally human even while taking on the role of a romantic heroine. She jokes with the soldiers—to her favorite saying, "I'll bet my head," one answers, "Which of your heads, pretty girl?" and she doesn't react in horror—and she confesses herself not as demure as one would expect: "I canna live wanting men. I would rather be a sparrow on the house-top, than live a woman without the company of men" (*3PW*, III, 61, 205). When she goes mad, after seeing the two men she loves first wound each other and then be slain by the English troops, and finally dies on their common grave, she represents not only the personal tragedy of an individual caught up in love and war, but the victim of the general madness, brutality, and horror of Culloden, of brother against brother, nation against nation.

In all Hogg's work, then—lyrics, reflective poems, moralities, tales, and long narratives—can be seen recurring methods and themes in the conventional forms. The emphasis on realistic details, especially from nature, the music of his rhythms, the drawing on personal experience or on tales and songs told him by his family, all indicate the folk poet drawing on the consciousness of his people and his region; the themes, too, with their focus on simple orthodox morality and on common-sense realism as opposed to chivalric fancy, also derive from this background. His treatments of women not just as victims or moral ideals, but as active and forceful participants in their own destinies, suggest an important corrective to the traditional Romantic heroine. Certainly, too, like many of his contemporaries, his purpose was to entertain, to sing a song to lift the spirit, to tell a story that excites the imagination, or to point a moral.

Yet, though the works seem conventional, Hogg generally infuses them with a certain flavor, as he suggests in the dedicatory poem to *The Brownie of Bodsbeck* when talking of the tales told in his cottage wherein was heard

> The bleat of mountain goat on high
> That from the cliff came quavering by;
> The echoing rock, the rushing flood,
> The cataract's swell, the moaning wood,
> That undefined and mingled hum—
> Voice of the desert never dumb,
> All these have left within this heart
> A feeling tongue can ne'er impart;
> A wildered and unearthly flame,
> A something that's without a name.
>
> (*Poems*, 386)

He lists these stories as "fairy tales of ancient time," religious tales, "scenes where martyrs bled," "the haunted dell," "the whispering wood,/And range of mountain solitude!" For what Hogg does in his best work is to infuse the conventional genres with his own personality. Most notably, he employs history, comedy, and the supernatural to impress the stamp of the "Ettrick Shepherd" on the stories and poems and raise them, generally, to a far higher level than that of his forgotten contemporaries. If his history was not always accurate, if his comedy sometimes upset the public taste, if the supernatural through overuse became occasionally self-parody, these elements nevertheless served to give new life to the conventions. Usually two, often all three, combine in his work, and they deserve further attention, as do the masterpieces of "Kilmeny," *Pilgrims of the Sun*, *The Poetic Mirror*, *The Brownie of Bodsbeck*, *The Confessions*, and a surprising number of other neglected tales and poems.

## CHAPTER 4

# History and Reality

T O be a Scot is to be immersed in history, for, in Scotland as in Faulkner's American South, "the past is never dead; it's not even past." Any nation or region threatened with assimilation by a more powerful and less tolerant neighbor must keep history and tradition alive as part of its survival; so the events of Scottish history greatly affect the Scottish present. Except for the contemporary first tale of *Three Perils of Woman*, all Hogg's extended narratives and the majority of his tales and poems deal with historical or prehistorical periods. Generally the most successful pieces take place during the times of the Covenanters in the late seventeenth century or of the Jacobite Rebellion of 1745. Hogg's use of history, however, differs considerably from Scott's scholarly approach, for the Shepherd once again presents folk truth and tradition rather than attempting factual accuracy. The great strength of Hogg's historical writings lies in his verisimilitude, achieved through a wide range of narrative techniques designed to impress the reader with the truth of his story. If that reader doesn't find himself in the actual historical period, he nevertheless finds himself in one exceedingly like it—fully believable and thus perhaps more real. Thus does art recreate history.

## I  The Use of History

Once again Hogg takes as his model Scott, who in the Waverley novels attempts to reconcile England and Scotland and achieves his aim both in the stories and in the popularity of the novels themselves. Hogg, like Scott, is at his best when dealing with events of the preceding century and a half; venturing to earlier times, even in Scotland, he produces a mixture of anachronism, fuzzy facts, and confused chronology. The long narratives most clearly illustrate these problems. *Queen Hynde* takes place, according to Thomas Thomson, in "that mythic period where poetry has free scope, and facts may be invented at pleasure . . . when the Scots were still a nation distinct from both Pict and Saxon" (*Poems*, 184); the poem, however, smacks more of Arthurian romance than barbaric realism, with its knights, chivalric code, and contests of strength. *The Three Perils of Man* takes place in the fourteenth century when Musgrave has taken Roxburgh for King Richard II of England. But Douglas Gifford shows how Hogg's siege actually combines the various attacks on Roxburgh over some 147 years:

Barbour's tale of how Douglas and his men took Roxburgh castle in 1314 doubtless suggested the final ruse of Hogg's narrative. . . . But the taking of castles in the period of Robert I was frequently attended with romantic detail which tradition would preserve for Hogg. Often chivalric conditions were agreed on by besiegers and besieged, as in Hogg's romance.

And just as Hogg conflates details from many historical and legendary sources to form the circumstances of his own siege of Roxburgh castle, the same procedure shows in his principal characters. His King Robert owes something to both Robert II and Robert III. His Earl of Douglas seems to be a blend in deed and character of many fourteenth-century Douglases.

Gifford also points out the anachronistic inclusion of Roger Bacon and Michael Scott (*3PM*, 468). *Mador*, of the works set in medieval times, perhaps succeeds historically because the allusions are so deliberately vague. Hogg never names the king as Robert II, and he changes the heroine's name from Elizabeth Muir to Ila Moore "on account of the rhythm" (*Poems*, 105). Only his note, that "the following poem is partly founded on an incident recorded in the Scottish annals of the fourteenth century" (105), alludes to a specific incident; the motif of the disguised king—traditionally referring to both James IV and James V and mentioned by Hogg in "The Bridal of Polmood" (*Tales*, 21)—tends to universalize the story rather than to specifically date it. The same pattern appears in the ballads, where only the outlines of the story have survived and the historical facts have been forgotten.

Hogg is usually more successful, though, with the comparatively recent principal events of Scottish history: the persecution of the Covenanters in the 1680s, the attempts to reestablish the Stuarts on the throne in 1715 and 1745, and the contemporary conflict with

Napoleon.[1] In dealing with these events, Hogg follows Scott's pattern of observing through the eyes of fictional characters; but he wishes not merely to depict historical actions and characters, but to show how those events affect the personal lives of the common people, as well as to present the views of such people, not academically historical views but painfully personal ones. The Culloden story in *Three Perils of Woman* shows how the events of history make heroes, then victims of the main characters, even though the battles themselves are not described.

Some of Hogg's best poetry consists of songs based on these historical events, and almost without exception they maintain the point of view of common soldiers or common people. The Shepherd's first success, "Donald M'Donald," tells of a young Highland soldier's loyalty to England whatever the past:

> What though we befriendit young Charlie?
>   To tell it I dinna think shame;
> Poor lad! he came to us but barely,
>   An' reckon'd our mountains his hame.
> 'Twas true that our reason forbade us,
>   But tenderness carried the day;
> Had Geordie come friendless amang us,
>   Wi' him we had a' gane away.
>     Sword an' buckler an' a',
>     Buckler an' sword an' a';
>     Now for George we'll encounter the devil,
>     Wi' sword an' buckler an' a'!

If Napoleon should invade, all the clans would rush to the defense —Gordons, Campbells, Grants, M'Kenzies, Murrays, Camerons, Stuarts, M'Leans, M'Kays—"An' I their gude-brither, M'Donald, /Shall ne'er be the last in the fray!/. . ./An' up wi' the bonnie blue bonnet,/The kilt an' the feather an' a'!'" (*Poems*, 283). The tuneful exuberance of the song reflects the enthusiasm of the youth, his idealism and even innocence. Hogg's most famous song, new words for a traditional melody in the *Jacobite Relics*, uses the lasses as speakers to show the romantic joy of the '45:

> 'Twas on a Monday morning,
>   Right early in the year,
> That Charlie come to our town,

                        The young Chevalier.
                      An' Charlie is my darling,
                        My darling, my darling,
                      Charlie is my darling,
                        The young Chevalier.

And each bonnie lassie sings, "Our king shall hae his ain again,/
An' Charlie is the man:/For Charlie he's my darling, etc." (*Poems*,
420).

   Yet Hogg shows the tragic aftermath as well as the romantic prelude. The defeated Callum-a-Glen, hunted by the "southern blood-
hounds," his sons slain and his daughter gone, still maintains his
faith and his iron will:

           The sun in his glory has look'd on our sorrow,
             The stars have wept blood over hamlet and lea;
           Oh! is there no day-spring for Scotland—no morrow
             Of bright renovation for souls of the free?
           Yes, One above all hath beheld our devotion,
             Our valour and faith are not hid from his ken;
           The day is abiding of stern retribution
             On all the proud foes of old Callum-a-Glen.

                                                    (*Poems*, 413)

The more conventional "Why Weeps yon Highland Maid?" nevertheless gains moving effect from the brief simplicity of the narrator's reply to the title question:

                   Stranger, that Highland plaid
                   Low in the dust was laid;
                   He who the relic wore,
                   He is, alas! no more:
                   He and his loyal clan were trodden
                   Down by slaves on dark Culloden.

                                                    (*Poems*, 418)

Hogg's personae, who convey timeless emotions if not always
contemporary accuracy, allow the poet himself to take a neutral
stand on historical events, a useful device to be discussed later.
Clearly, though, his interest always lies with the individual and
not with the event.

   One of Hogg's most characteristic and effective historical

poems is "The Field of Waterloo," and a comparison of it with
Scott's self-confessedly weak poem of the same title clearly shows
the difference between their approaches. Scott's poem is a meditation: a descriptive tour of the battlefield, a recounting of battle
scenes, and a final tribute to the dead, followed by patriotic praise
of Britain for, like Saint George, having faced a dragon and
"quell'd devouring pride, and vindicated right." Hogg's poem,
on the other hand, takes the dramatic form, recounting a conversation that takes place the evening after the battle between a
mortally wounded Scot and two European soldiers who "paused
to view/The havoc done on Waterloo." Their talk occurs amid
realistic postbattle horrors:

> every moan was heard as near,
> And every plaint fell on the ear;
> The parting throb, the smothered sigh,
> And shriek of sharpest agony:
> But every anathema said
> By widowed dame and weeping maid,
> Or passed in soldier's dying groan,
> All cursed one, and one alone. . . .
> But all was sorrow and lament—
> Or weeping for the valiant dead,
> Or curses on a tyrant's head.
>
> (*Poems*, 333)

The Prussian and the Russian ask about the day, and the Scot
calls it the greatest battle since Bannockburn. The visitors protest
that they have witnessed greater battles—Leipzig and Borodino—
and state their cases with graphic details, but the Scot maintains
the importance of Waterloo, arguing that Britain's intervention
constituted true bravery and friendship. "You fought for home,"
says the Scot; "you fought for life,/For monarch, kinsmen,
children, wife," and when the Prussian agrees that all these were
at stake, the Scot argues,

> The less your merit and your meed,
> 'Twas desperation did the deed;
> And where's the creature forced to strife
> That will not fight for breath and life?
> The hunted deer can hold at bay

> The gallant hound—yet who will say
> The deer is brave.

Britain, on the other hand, secure and free over the sea, fought
only for the cause of human right, and the Scot concludes,

> To fight for life I count it nought.
> But he who, seeing friend o'erthrown
> By sordid guile, and trodden down,
> Flies to his aid, and ventures all
> At friendship's and at honour's call;
> And, by his blood and jeopardy,
> Succeeds, and sets the injured free—
> This, this, I say, is bravery!''

The Prussian, "a stoic cool," agrees, then speaks "in earnest
way,/Of things unfitting poet's lay," of needful waste of life, of
politics, and similar conventional sentiments; the Russian attributes the victory to God and Prince Alexander; but the dying Scot
has the last words: a prayer thanking God for the victory and
asking Him to protect his wife and parents. This prayer of complete acceptance and trust in the power and will of God—its
simple Christian faith—moves even the Prussian disciple of
Voltaire. The poem ends with a narrator explaining how he visits
the widow's cottage and seems to see evidence of the guardian
spirit which the soldier had prayed for. By focusing on the human
and specific rather than the abstract and meditative, Hogg gains
immediacy and realism where Scott produces only a laureatelike
lay. Hogg presents both the personal and the national, shows both
the victory and the price of victory, where Scott presents only
words. In short, Hogg creates a fictional reality, Scott only
rhetoric.
    Differences between the two men's historical narratives can also
be seen in Hogg's superb *Brownie of Bodsbeck*, which, like the
Culloden story of *Three Perils of Woman*, uses historical events
as an integral part of the tale. Hogg's treatment of the events,
however, led to a dispute with Scott over historical method. Set in
the autumn of 1685, the *Brownie* concerns Walter Laidlaw of
Chapelhope and his daughter, Katharine, who has been giving aid
to Covenanters hiding from John Graham of Claverhouse, the

commander of the English troops. Since the military defeat of the Covenanters—mainly Presbyterians protesting Charles II's attempts to establish a state-controlled church—at Bothwell Bridge in 1679, they had been hunted down and forced to swear allegiance or be executed for treason; the persecution continued for several years, and the fanatical brutality was not unlike the massacre of the clans after Culloden some sixty years later. Though Hogg's narrative centers on Walter's family and a mysterious goblin, the Brownie, who protects them, the historical background, especially the character of Claverhouse, is crucial to both the story and the dispute with the author of *Old Mortality*.

In Scott's novel, Claverhouse, though presented as a fanatic, nevertheless represents the aristocratic sense of order, in opposition to Balfour of Burley, an assassin and leader of the Covenanters. Claverhouse tells the hero, Morton, "We are both fanatics; but there is some distinction between the fanaticism of honour and that of dark and sullen superstition." Like Burley, the Englishman kills "without mercy or remorse," but he explains, "There is a difference, I trust, between the blood of learned and reverend prelates and scholars, of gallant soldiers and noble gentlemen, and the red puddle that stagnates in the veins of psalm-singing mechanics, crack-brained demagogues, and sullen boors."[2] Though feeling no compassion for the lower classes, Claverhouse emerges as the visible power of order and law. Given Scott's own views of history and his fears of French Revolutionary movements in England, it must be conceded that the English viscount represents a necessary, if extreme force in the maintenance of order.

Not so the Clavers of *Brownie*, for Hogg uses the "detested" nickname given Graham by the people. The Shepherd's tale derives, as he says, from the historian Wodrow, with the local part "from the relation of my own father, who had the best possible traditionary account of the incidents" (*Tales*, 1). Although Hogg's assertions of truth are often suspect, the story does indeed present a quite different picture of Graham, one seen from the point of view of the persecuted as well as of those, like Walter, attempting to remain neutral. Hogg himself, somewhat uncharacteristically, makes no attempt to remain impartial, as he tells, in the background Chapter 2, how Clavers "let loose his savage troopers upon those peaceful districts, with peremptory orders to plunder, waste, disperse, and destroy the conventiclers, wherever they might be found" (4). After the mysterious slaughter of five of his men, "Clavers is said to have broke out into the most violent rage, and to have sworn that night by the Blessed Virgin and all the Holy Trinity, utterly to extirpate the seed of the whining psalm-singing race from the face of the earth, and that ere Beltein there should not be as much Whig blood in Scotland as would make a dish of soup to a dog. He, however, concealed from the privy council the loss of these five men, nor did they ever know of it to this day" (6). When Clavers comes to Chapelhope and sees Katharine apparently at devotions, he and one of his men grab her "in the rudest manner," only to be interrupted by the return of Walter, who finds her "singing . . . within the grasp of the gentle and virtuous Clavers." Walter "was at least a foot taller," Hogg writes, "than any of them, and nearly as wide round the chest as both of them. In one moment his immense fingers grasped both their slender necks, almost meeting behind each of their windpipes" (19). On recovering, however, Clavers has Walter arrested. In the next episode, when Katharine is almost raped by a hypocritical curate and is saved by the Brownie, Hogg draws a parallel between the curate and Clavers—they practice the same religion, exercise the same total authority, and use public beliefs for private satisfaction (seduction on the one hand, vengeance on the other)—and the terms "gentle and virtuous" become even more ironic.

Yet when Hogg's novel appeared, according to the *Familiar Anecdotes*, Scott disapproved, "his shaggy eyebrows . . . hanging very sore down, a bad prelude, which I knew too well." Hogg defended himself against the expected charge of imitation by pointing out how the manuscript of *Brownie* had been finished before the appearance of *Old Mortality*, but Scott shrugged off that similarity, objecting instead to the "false and unfair picture of the times and the existing characters altogether. An exaggerated and unfair picture!" He continued, "I only tell you that with the exception of Old Nanny the crop-eared Covenanter who is by far the best character you ever drew in your life I dislike the tale exceedingly and assure you it is a distorted a prejudiced and untrue picture of the Royal party." But Hogg replied in a huff, "It is a devilish deal truer than your's though; and on that ground I make my appeal to my country" (*FA*, 106-107).

Hogg does have the last word, for in a later introduction to the *Brownie* he writes, "On the publication of the first edition, I was grievously blamed, by a certain party, for having drawn an unfair character of Clavers. I can only say that it is the character I had heard drawn of him all my life, and the character of him which was impressed upon my mind since my earliest remembrance, which all his eulogists can never erase. Moreover, I have not contrived one incident in order to make his character blacker than it was: I may have taken a few of the worst, and condensed them, and that is all, and perfectly fair. If, through all the histories of that suffering period, I had discovered one redeeming quality about Clavers, I would have brought it forward, but I found none. He had the nature of a wolf, and the bravery of a bull-dog" (*Tales*, 2). Hogg never had Scott's historical overview or purpose, but his presentations of the folk traditions provide an equally revealing look at historical events. In taking the people's point of view, Hogg presents a humanly convincing picture that itself makes an important contribution to the record of events.

## II  *Narrative Devices*

The historical works—with their explicit protestations of accuracy (often belied by the actual treatment of events)—raise the question of how Hogg achieves his illusion of reality. The verisimilitude necessary to give a sense of historical reality becomes even more crucial in the supernatural stories. Hogg's use of various narrative techniques to increase the sense of truth marks perhaps his greatest literary sophistication. Earlier novelists had used many tricks: Defoe and Fielding insist on their works as histories, emphasized by the piling up of detail; Richardson and Smollett employ the epistolary form and put themselves forward as mere editors of "facts"; even Scott often (and often embarrassingly) uses a frame-story narrator to tell the main story. The Gothic novelists, especially, did much with the possibilities of narration, as they attempted to find convincing ways of presenting fantastic events: hence the discovered manuscript, the letters, the series of narrators, all designed to distance the events from present-day rationalism.

Hogg uses most of the devices of his predecessors, but with even more insistence on the literal truth of his tales and poems.

His chief method was to write autobiographically, either in the character of the "Ettrick Shepherd," as created by himself and by Wilson in the *Noctes*, or in an often satiric persona. The tales often start out like the sketches, with Hogg recounting events he has heard about. Like Fielding, too, who talked with Sophie Western, Hogg tells of visiting his fictional characters, or their graves, or other visible signs of their habitation. In most of these instances, the "I," the poet, and the real Hogg are almost indistinguishable from one another.

With the character of the Spy in his newspaper, however, Hogg begins to employ a clearer fictional persona, though one still resembling the author. The Spy describes himself as a "bachelor, about sixty years of age [who has] spent the most of my days in the country, where I have been engaged in innumerable projects, which have all miscarried: but nothing in the world disturbs or perplexes me. My mind is so buoyant, and my thoughts so vague that if I can get a few of my fellow-creatures, placed before my eyes, that I may contemplate their various manners and looks, it is sufficient for me: I can laugh at their follies, weep over their misfortunes, and feel as deeply for all their concerns as they can possibly do themselves." Except for the age being twenty years off, the picture is identical to that revealed in his letters. The Spy continues, describing himself as just a simple man who has only left the mountains a few years ago; hence, everything will be quite new, and "any incongruity of taste or character will be much more ready to strike me, than such as have been used to witness the same scenes all their days" (*Spy*, 1-2). Both the freshness of *The Spy* and the problems of impropriety derive from his supposedly naive reactions to city life.

From this semiautobiographical observer, it is but another brief shift to the creation of a first-person narrator who is the main character of a story, as in Defoe's fictional autobiographies. Fine examples can be found in several of Hogg's tales, including "The Adventures of Basil Lee," where the title character writes his life story for a moral purpose, again like Defoe's creations. Basil offers his story not "as a model to be copied, but as one to be avoided; and may those who laugh at my inconsistencies learn from them to steer a different course" (*Tales*, 237). Yet the moral tone is even less convincing than Moll Flanders's, for Basil merely cautions against impatiently changing professions. Basil's many occupations—farmer, shepherd, barman, merchant, gigolo, and soldier in Scotland and North America—are mere pegs on which to hang a picaresque novel full of bawdy life and antiromance, in which the hero and a very lively heroine named Clifford (no mean picaroon herself) finally achieve a happy marriage of eighteen years, albeit a rather "dissipated, confused, irregular sort of life" (*Tales*, 265). Another common device, the letter to Hogg then passed on to his readers of both *The Spy* and *Blackwood's*, led to fine "factual" tales such as the Poe-esque "Strange Letter of a Lunatic" and the hoax of "The Pongos," a story of a South African tribe of half-men, half-beasts. Near-hoaxes, in fact, result easily from such techniques, and one of Hogg's best, "The Surpassing Adventures of Allan Gordon," makes use of a schoolmaster's transcript of the hero's adventures near the North Pole. This contribution to popular accounts of polar exploration includes the hero's relationship with a polar bear, Nancy, who becomes jealous of his native wife and mistresses.[3]

Whoever the narrator, however, Hogg buttresses his stories with direct appeals to reality. As in the autobiographies he mixes large doses of fiction with fact, so in the tales and poems he adds large doses of fact to the fancy. Hogg becomes so perplexed, for example, with the "Strange Letter" that he writes a friend for further information and prints the reply, from Alexander Walker, dated Crowell, 6 November 1827, which confirms some of the story but also adds further mystery. Basil Lee begins his tale much like Lemuel Gulliver—"I was third son to a respectable farmer in the upper parts of Berwickshire"—before moving on to his fantastic globe-spanning adventures. Finally, of course, Hogg introduces as evidence his own experiences, as well as letters, journals, and books which may or may not exist. The *Brownie* ends with Hogg suggesting that "if there are any incidents in this tale that may still appear a little mysterious, they will all be rendered obvious by turning to a pamphlet entitled, '*A Cameronian's Tale*, or the Life of John Brown, written by himself.' But any reader of common ingenuity may very easily solve them all"; this publication, however, apparently does not exist (*Tales*, 61).

One appealing method by which Hogg adds to the reality of his stories is the inclusion of his contemporaries, even apart from historical figures who appear. In *Three Perils of Woman*, Gatty pursues her Edinburgh education by going to a play where she sits opposite Walter Scott and one of his daughters, "dressed with simplicity and good taste." Scott, she reports, was exceedingly good-looking, and watched the players "out at the tail of his eye, as if he deemed it all a joke" (*3PW*, I, 103-104). Earlier, her father had seen Scott in Parliament, describing him as "a carl that sits always with his right shoulder to you, with hair of a pale silver grey, a head like a tower, braid shoulders, and long shaggy e'e-brees—the very picture of an auld, gruff Border Baron." Daniel Bell won't provide an introduction to Scott, however, for the great man is probably "pestered to death wi' introductions of sentimental muses, would-be poets, and puppy nobility and gentry" (I, 30-31). Hogg's conclusion to a fine fairy tale, "The Hunt of Eildon," also employs this device in a grotesque comic effect. After being saved by being changed into a beautiful moorfowl, the heroine is shot by a hunter and sent to his Edinburgh friend, "at whose table she was divided and eaten, on the 20th of October, 1817" (*Tales*, 235). The fate of his heroine might seem incongruous, except for the humor of the story in other respects, much of which also turns on eating, as well as on Hogg's typical undercutting of romantic conclusions, in *Hynde* and *Three Perils of Man*, for instance. The *Confessions*, as will be seen later, remains Hogg's most impressive use of narrative variation with its three-part pattern of editor's narrative, main character's confessions, and final contemporary account.

Two other successful and characteristic narrative techniques include the uses of dialogue, often in dialect, and of frame-stories. Dialogue to set and even to tell a story occurs in both the prose and poetry, as it does in the sketches. In "The Frazers in the Correi," for example, Hogg sketches the whole aftermath of Culloden in the dialogue between an old man and a young girl which tells of her family being forced to hide from the pursuing English. The ballad "Bothwell Brigg," commemorating the defeat of the Covenanters, consists of a talk between Janet and a noblewoman who had visited the scene of battle, found the girl's sorely wounded husband, and nursed him back to health. But the Lady graphically pictures the wounded men and the husband's near death before the final moral, which gains emphasis from being the characters' conclusions rather than those of an omniscient narrator. Janet tells her anti-Covenant Lady,

> If good deeds count in heaven, ladye,
> Eternal bliss to share,
> Ye hae done a deed will save your soul,
> Though ye should never do mair.

And the lady replies,

> Get up, get up, my kind Janet,
> But never trow tongue or pen,
> That a' the world are lost to good,
> Except the Covenant men.
>
> (*Poems*, 357)

Hogg, though clearly sympathetic to the Covenanters' cause, can remain objective about the historical event and look at the results of the battle and the need for tolerance on both sides. The dialogue intensifies both the reality and the humanity.

Comic uses of the technique, besides the humor of the dialect, involve the ironic contrasts between the two speakers, where often one's realism undercuts the other's rhetorical flights. The narrator of "Ringan and May," for example, asks her lover about the laverock's (lark's) song, and he interprets it as a seduction song. She runs away, properly shocked, but concludes,

> for all the sturt and strife I made;
> For all I did, and all I said,
> Alas! I fear it will be lang
> Or I forget that wee burd's sang!
> And langer still or I can flee
> The lad that told that sang to me!
>
> (*Poems*, 343-44)

Many tales, too, open *in medias res* with a dialogue, often between two shepherds discussing strange events or ideas. The beginning of "Sound Morality" is typical:

"It is a grand thing, true and genuine morality! If I were a minister, I wad never preach up onything but just pure morality," said Cuddy Cauldrife to his neighbour shepherd, Michael Moody, one morning as they sat on the top of Lochfell, and cast their eyes over the fair dales of the West Border.

"An' what for wad ye no be preaching aught but morality, Cuddy? We hae muckle need o' hearing some other sort o' doctrine than cauld morality, an' to hae some other thing to put our trust in too, beside that." (*Tales*, 200)

After some further discussion, Cuddy relates an undistinguished tale of an innkeeper's natural goodness and a minister's neglect. Sometimes the dialogue continues through an entire story, though usually it sets the scene and characters, and is followed by a third-person narrator. Even the *Brownie* begins dramatically with a dialogue, between Walter and his wife, before the historical explanation of the second chapter. Such dialogues provide, especially in the ghostly tales, the point of view of the common people, with all their sincerity, simplicity, and common sense. Such openings also remove Hogg from overt involvement in the story, preserving his neutrality as merely an editor or observer not accountable for the content. Often, however, the discussions are more interesting than the tales eventually told, although occasionally the characters of the dialogue do become principal figures in the story, especially if it concerns the seeing of ghosts. In all cases, however, they help establish the reality.

The frame-story device is less common, since it needs a longer work to be completely effective, but *Three Perils of Man* and *The Queen's Wake* show Hogg's mastery of the technique. In the novel, the company calling on Michael Scott becomes trapped in his castle, with the wizard himself as a hostage. While waiting for help, and without food, they hold a contest with the teller of the best tale to win the maiden, Delany; the loser, however, shall, "if need require it, be blooded and flayed in this same chamber for food to his associates" (*3PM*, 203). The five stories, all autobiographical and interlocking in ways the narrators hadn't expected, take up nearly a hundred pages. Each tale is told in a characteristic style: the friar speaks in biblical form, with each sentence numbered and separately paragraphed; Gibbie, the good-humored Laird of Peatstacknowe, tells a comic story revolving around food, to which the poet objects on account of its being too close to their immediate situation; Charlie Scott recounts a dialect tale of warfare and bravery in keeping with his simple tastes and abilities, but Tam Craik objects to its length, confusion, abrupt ending, and endless anecdotes (charges that could be brought against Hogg himself); Tam, however, turns out to be the subject of Gibbie's tale, and he finishes off the history of his life. The poet recites his poem, "When the Kye comes Hame," but due to drink and a fuzzy memory can only sing seven of the sixteen verses; he finally tells the highly moral story of "The Three Sisters" in prose. The listeners judge on the basis of temperament —Michael Scott, for instance, doesn't care much for tales of Christian martyrdom and faith—though the wizard declares that Charlie should win. They determine to draw lots, however, rather than to decide on the worst story, but are saved by troopers before the loser, Gibbie, must suffer the final sacrifice, much to the dismay of the gluttonous Tam, who had "put forth his forefinger to ascertain the thickness of fat on the laird's ribs" (*3PM*, 321). Though the tales themselves add little to the novel as a whole, they provide an entertaining interlude in addition to commenting morally or comically on the characters of the tellers.

Hogg's best use of the frame-story, as well as one of his best historical pictures, occurs in *The Queen's Wake*, where the frame contains as much interest as many of the inset poems. The poem's premise is a contest of minstrels held on the occasion of Queen Mary's return to the Scotland of 1561, torn by civil strife and praying for the return of peace and order. The summer passes with no relief until finally "rang the shouts from tower and tree/ That Scotland's queen was on the sea," and

> Each bard attuned the loyal lay,
> And for Dunedin hied away; . . .
> The chiefs forsook their ladies fair,
> The priest his beads and books of prayer;
> The farmer left his harvest day,
> The shepherd all his flocks to stray;
> The forester forsook the wood,
> And hasted on to Holyrood.
>
> (*Poems*, 3)

At the palace they see the fair, young queen "Driven from her home, a helpless child/. . ./In one short year her hopes all crossed—/A parent, husband, kingdom lost" (3). She responds to this grand reception and especially to an old minstrel's simple song which prophesies her doom. Enchanted, wishing to prove

"the wondrous powers of Scottish song," she commands all the
bards to attend the palace on Christmas week to sing for her,
neither ribaldry nor jest, "nor adulation bland,/But legends of
our native land" (5). At the appointed time, a horde of minstrels
arrives, and after a great feast they enter the overwhelming
presence of Mary:

> Oft the rapt bard had thought alone,
> Of charms by mankind never known,
> Of virgins, pure as opening day,
> Or bosom of the flower of May;
> Oft dreamed of being free from stain,
> Of maidens of the emerald main,
> Of fairy dames in grove at even,
> Of angels in the walks of heaven:
> But, nor in earth, the sea, nor sky,
> In fairy dream nor fancy's eye,
> Vision his soul had ever seen
> Like Mary Stuart, Scotland's queen.
>
> (7)

In this introduction, Hogg sets the nationalistic tone of the
poem—the Wake will not only educate the young queen, with
minstrels in their native dress arriving from all regions of the
country, but it will enlighten the reader with a collection of
regional ballads and legends which will demonstrate the strength,
variety, and power of Scottish song and story.

The contest begins, not improbably, with a song by the queen's
favorite, the Italian Rizzio, "though unskilled in Scottish song."
His conventional, sentimental romance, however, wins little favor
from the other listeners, who "admired, but loved not much, his
song"; they think the foreigner had but "mimicked passion, woe,
and pain," and a Highland chieftain becomes especially incensed
"that song so vapid, artful, terse,/Should e'er compete with
Scottish verse" (9). Mary, being used to Continental minstrelsy,
approves Rizzio's effort, but next comes a true Scot, the sixty-
year-old Gardyn, who

> Stately . . . strode, nor bow made he,
> Not even a look of courtesy.
> The simpering cringe, and fawning look,

> Of him who late the lists forsook,
> Roused his proud heart, and fired his eye,
> That glowed with native dignity.
>                                                    (9)

Gardyn sings the "wild and dreadful song" of "Young Kennedy,"
and the procession of bards continues, from Ettrick, from the
West coast, from the country of the Dee, from Leven, from Fife,
so many, in fact, that the names of some don't survive, according
to the narrator. In all, seventeen poems appear, including two
masterpieces—the comic "Witch of Fife" and the haunting
"Kilmeny"—and such powerful narratives as "Glen-Avin" and
"Abbot M'Kinnon." Not only does Hogg provide appropriate
materials for the minstrels depending on their regions and backgrounds, but he distinguishes among each singer in character and
dress. Each becomes both a type *and* an individual.

Finally the time arrives for Mary to award the prize, a splendid
harp. Among the first night's singers, Gardyn wins by a single
vote, but Queen Mary, angered that Rizzio was beaten, calls for a
recount, whereupon the Italian receives fewer votes than before,
and Mary learns the independent nature of her subjects. The bard
of Ettrick defeats the second night's singers, and a nameless youth
from the Lowlands those of the third, much to the anger of some
Highlanders. The gathering threatens to erupt into a violent contention between Highland and Border minstrels, but the youth
refuses to sing again, so Gardyn and the Ettrick bard are left to
contend for the prize. Gardyn wins and bears away the gem- and
gold-encrusted harp to the Highlands, where, according to Hogg's
notes, it was found some two hundred years later. The loser
requests a harp also and receives one, not of rich and curious
workmanship, but one fashioned by a wizard which "will not
yield one measure bland/Beneath a skilless stranger hand," but
will produce a magic sound by those who can find its power. The
poem ends with the rediscovery of this magic Caledonian harp by
Walter Scott himself, who

> screwed the chords, he tried a strain;
> 'Twas wild—he tuned and tried again,
> Then poured the numbers bold and free,
> The ancient magic melody.

So charmed, "Even fairies sought our land again,/So powerful was the magic strain" (57-58). Scott points out the harp to Hogg, who takes it to his mountains and "taught the wandering winds to sing" (59). That none of the best poems of *The Queen's Wake* wins a prize may be a comment on literary criticism, however, just as the treatments of Rizzio and of Mary's coming to understand the Scots through poetry are comments on history and art.

*The Queen's Wake* contains a truly representative variety of Hogg's work. Based on history, it uses traditional forms, includes songs and ballads, and tells stories ranging from the purely comic to the horrific. Had he written only this book and the other works mentioned in the last two chapters, Hogg's achievement would have ensured his place as a minor poet—as indeed it did, for *The Queen's Wake* was the book on which his early reputation rested. Yet its two best poems indicate the chief elements which would raise his works above mere competence: comedy and the supernatural, which, in conjunction with his technical proficiency in the telling of stories, often give significant meaning to his work. If the bard of Ettrick only placed second under Queen Mary, it was at least higher than all but one of the other minstrels; if Hogg declines to give himself the chief prize, he nevertheless knows his worth.

# CHAPTER 5

# *The Comic Spirit*

TO say that Hogg has a comic view of life would be to credit him with an intellectual viewpoint that he himself would make fun of. Yet comedy plays a major part in his works, even serious or tragic ones. The comedy derives, like most other aspects of his writing, from his character—good-natured, exuberant, sometimes bawdy—and from his background, as it realistically undercuts romantic and sentimental tendencies. Many subplots of the longer works—Wene's flirtations in *Hynde*, Charlie's adventures in *Three Perils of Man*, even Wringhim's upbringing in the *Confessions*—turn on comic, often farcical incidents. For Hogg's humor is nothing if not broad: he works in burlesque, satire, and parody. Nearly all the comic pieces are enormously entertaining; but the satiric pieces go further, revealing Hogg's criticisms of modern society, the sophisticated world which he forsook for the homely comforts of Altrive Lake; and the parodies of *The Poetic Mirror* indicate the triumph of his imitative technique.

The humorous writings, however, often came under attack for streaks of eighteenth-century bawdiness. A *Blackwood's* review of *Winter Evening Tales* noted "an occasional coarseness—we had almost said grossness . . . which half an hour judiciously spent in correction might have removed. Mr. Hogg . . . is too fond of calling some things by their plain names, which would be better expressed by circumlocution; and now and then he betrays what we shall at once call, *vulgarity*."[1] Some scenes, such as an extended search by a cuckolded husband for his new bride and her lover in "The Bridal of Polmood," seem directly transferred from conventional farce. Others, which turn on realistic details usually involving sex or food, mark Hogg's feelings for the earthy enjoy-

ment of simple pleasures. In his *Memoirs* Hogg recognizes the
"blunt rusticity" of the tales, but defends them, for

> they appeared not only more characteristic of the life that I then led, but
> also of the manners that I was describing. As to the indelicacies . . . I do
> declare that such a thought never entered into my mind, so that the public
> are indebted for these indelicacies to the acuteness of the discoverers. Wo
> be to that reader who goes over a simple and interesting tale fishing for
> indelicacies, without calculating on what is natural for the characters with
> whom he is conversing; a practice, however, too common among people
> of the present age, especially if the author be not a blue-stocking. . . . I
> am certain I never intentionally meant ill, and that I hope to be forgiven,
> both by God and man, for every line that I have written injurious to the
> cause of religion, or virtue, or of good manners.

His final answer to the charge of earthiness in the tales is forthright: "I liked them the better for it, and altered nothing" (*Mem*,
50). Although he did make some revisions in collected editions,
happily the comedy, with its bawdiness, remains; and it remains
alive.

## I  *Burlesque*

When Hogg attempts purely comic pieces, his broad humor so
takes over that he creates a burlesque more successful than the
conventional form with which he begins. Of the main types of his
writing—songs, epic, historical adventure, ballad—there is hardly
one that he doesn't subject to a burlesque treatment that results in
some of his most effective work; indeed, "Basil Lee" and "The
Witch of Fife" stand among his major accomplishments.

The most common comic effect in the burlesque songs is exaggeration of the dialect. Hogg also maintains the countryman's
point of view, so that his characters become even more free with
their tongues and more disrespectful of authority. "Up an' rin
awa', Geordie," an answer to a Whig song of 1746, repeats the
king's name familiarly and insultingly every other line to empha-
size the cowardice of the king and his troops:

> Up an' rin awa', Geordie,
> Up an' rin awa', Geordie,
> For feint a stand in Cumberland

> Your troops can mak ava, Geordie.
> Your bauld militia are in qualms,
>     In ague fits an' a', Geordie,
> And auntie Wade, wi' pick an' spade,
>     Is delving through the snaw, Geordie.

Nor does the speaker hesitate to attack on a personal level:

> That Hanover's a dainty place,
>     It suits you to a straw, Geordie,
> Where ane may tame a buxom dame,
>     An' chain her to a wa', Geordie.
> An' there a man may burn his cap,
>     His hat, an' wig, an' a', Geordie;
> They're a' sae daft, your scanty wits
>     Will ne'er be miss'd awa, Geordie.
>
> (*Poems*, 362-63)

Another drinking song, this time praising the contemporary William IV, contains a similar speaker—irreverent, unpolished, and exuberant:

> Oh, Willie was a wanton wag,
>     The blithest lad that e'er I saw;
> He 'mang the lasses bure the brag,
>     An' carried aye the gree awa'. . . .
>
> Though now he wears the British crown,
>     For whilk he never cared a flee—
> Yet still the downright honest tar,
>     The same kind-hearted chield is he. . . .
>
> I've ae advice to gie my king,
>     An' that I'll gie wi' right good-will;
> Stick by the auld friends o' the crown,
>     Wha bore it up through good an' ill.
>
> (*Poems*, 433)

These two songs make fun of such as "Donald M'Donald," while a fine mock-epic spoofs Hogg's journeys to other worlds. "The Russiadde," a fragment of an ancient epic purportedly

written by Gilbert Hume, a Selkirk souter or shoemaker, begins
with comic rhymes and alliteration:

> A song of sooth and sober sadness,
> Of matchless might and motley madness,
> Long as the reach of morning lingle,
> And brisk as blaze of evening ingle,
> Begin, my Borough Muse, and sing.

The poet then invokes the detested Virgil:

> Genius of Virgil, here inspire me,
> That men may read, though not admire me!
> Of every method of description,
> In verse, or prose, without restriction,
> For saying most, and telling least,
> Thine is the easiest and the best.

Though the comment is Hume's, it smacks of Hogg's constant
condemnations of classical learning and teaching.

After 150 lines of digression, Hume protests to his "prosing
muse" that he's achieved only one good line: "In Selkirk once
there lived a man." The muse apologizes and, since she hates
"description's meagre art,/And love[s] a tale with all my heart,"
begins her true story of Russell, an heroic warrior, whose most
impressive exploits involve women, since "Myriads of fair he
overcame;/And then for children (precious things)/He beat the
Turks or Persian kings." He receives his comeuppance, however,
when two sisters bear his latest children, and the church, the law,
and the entire village become outraged. Lady Coom, his patron's
wife, who has more than a dispassionate interest in Russ, gives
him horse and armor, and the hero flees; but he stops after only
three miles to dally with a country wench, and the next morning
his pursuers catch up. An epic battle ensues, with Russ using "a
lean and sordid priest" to club his enemies down. Hume inter-
polates, "Now, gallant Muse, I think thou'lt show 'em/Thou
can'st indite heroic poem," but as thousands of pursuers close in,
Russ seems doomed until Venus casts a pitying eye and comes to
his rescue. Beautiful she is, and highly rhetorical as well, but her
offer to take him to see many wonders fails to interest the hero,
for

> Russell's dull reason found her household
> Of crude ideas all bamboozled:
> Of all that speech, from end to end,
> One word he could not comprehend;

so Venus throws him over her shoulders, clasps his fists on her breasts, and flies off through a thunderstorm described in war imagery that makes Virgil a "prosing drivelling fool" (*Poems,* 294-300). They see visions of hell and of heaven, until finally she takes him underneath the sea, though scenes there must await the unwritten Book Two. "The Russiadde" burlesques not only epic style and other-worldly visions but even Hogg's seduction stories, while the hero, with his exaggerated prowess and stupidity, and the poet, with his contempt for art demonstrated in both comments and practice, undercut the typical romantic attitudes.

Burlesque elements also inform many of the straight historical adventures, including "Sir Simon Brodie" and "Basil Lee." The former reverses the typical form by making the comic buffoon the main character and relegating the love story and the historical background to the subplot. "Dressed in a fantastic old style, and armed with a long sword having a gold handle," Sir Simon— "enthusiastically, madly loyal [with] no sophistication in [his] character"[2]—charges about in defense of King Charles's cause. Thrown off a ship by his enemies, Sir Simon is about to drown, but "a mermaid made up to him, or some sort of large seal which he took for one, and the creature taking Sir Simon for a male of the same species, became very teasing and familiar with him" (245). But when he asks, "Are you for the king or the parliament?" (245-46), she shakes her head, so he takes her prisoner. Finally, abandoned on a desolate island, he encounters an eight-foot corpse whom he also challenges. "I am for the church invisible," the figure replies, and runs away before the knight can run it through. The story ends rather abruptly and weakly, however, like so many of Hogg's tales. That the mermaid and the ghost have realistic explanations only adds to the exaggeration by suggesting that such a character as Sir Simon might exist. Hogg fails to create the depth of a Falstaff because of his hero's absurd monomania and "opaque intellect," but the story itself serves as a burlesque contrast to the other straightforward historical pieces which make up the *Tales of the Wars of Montrose.*

Probably the most coherent of all Hogg's historical burlesques is "Basil Lee," which also develops most of his main themes in addition to exaggerating the Defoe-like realistic adventure story. After a matter-of-fact description of his background and education, Basil tells of his first misfortunes: the several occupations that work against his desire for a life of idle pleasure. Happily, however, he manages to fail as joiner, ploughman, shepherd, merchant, and farmer. His experiences as a shepherd clearly show Hogg's method of undercutting the romantic view; Basil "entered upon this celebrated classical employment with raptures of delight. Never had a mortal such a charming prospect of true felicity! I rejoiced in the opportunity that it would afford me of reading so many delightful books, learning so many fine songs and tunes, of which I was passionately fond, and above all, of taking Jessy below my plaid" (*Tales*, 238). This pastoral dream doesn't work out, however, because the sheep wander, the dogs don't respect him, and the servant girl Jessy, after one or two unfortunate experiences, sends a ragamuffin boy with Basil's dinner instead of bringing it herself. Moreover, Basil reports, "I was exposed to cold, to snow and rain, and all manner of hardships. In short, before the first half year had expired, I had fairly come to the conclusion, that the life of a shepherd, instead of being the most delightful and romantic, was the most dull and wretched state of existence" (239). As a merchant, though, Basil proves equally incompetent, selling a family cut tobacco for tea and serving a Highlander vitriol instead of whisky. In the latter case,

he drank it off, and went away without any remark, save that "she was te cood"; but, when he left the shop, I observed that his lips were primmed close together, and the tears were streaming over his cheeks. On examining the bottle I discovered my mistake, and had no doubt that the man would die instantly. . . . Day came after day, and no word arrived of the dead Highland drover; till, at length, about a month after, I was thunderstruck at seeing the same old man enter the shop, and again ask me to sell him "a glassfu' of te whisky." I could not believe my eyes; but he removed all my doubts, by adding, "an' it pe your vill, let her have te same tat she got fan she vas here pefore." I said I feared I had none of that now, but that some alleged it was not quite the thing. "Hech, man, she shoorly vas te cood!" replied he, "for hit no pe little tat mak auld

Tonald pegh (pant), an py cot she vas mhait and trink to hersel for two wheeks.'' (240)

Basil succeeds somewhat better as a soldier, despite his arrant cowardice, and the middle third of the story concerns his adventures with British forces in the American Revolution. En route to Canada, he takes away a lieutenant's beautiful companion, Clifford Mackay, and must fight a duel. After dismissing various dangerous weapons, he chooses small swords as apparently the best means of defending himself. The duel becomes a mockery of the honorable affair originally intended, for Basil aims only at keeping himself from injury, holding ''my arm at full stretch, crossing my sword before me, and making it ply up and down with the swiftness of lightning'' (245). Accidentally wounded, Lt. Frazer becomes incensed and pins him to the ground through the cheek, but Basil ''wounded him in behind, sticking my sword directly in a part of his body which I do not choose to name.'' Both men then receive treatment from ''a farrier, that bled American horses, men, and women, alternately, as occasion required'' (246). In a final twist, Clifford, the object of the duel, turns out to be an Inverness streetwalker who becomes Basil's mistress for the next few years.

Basil's instinct for survival also colors his detailed descriptions of battle. With the attacking troops completely exposed to American cannon, Basil fervently wishes ''to have been on some other service; or, by some means, have avoided going up that hill! I am not sure but that I looked for some opportunity of skulking, but I looked in vain; and it was not even possible for me to fall down among the dead, for as yet no one had fallen.'' Almost immediately, however, two men next to him fall, ''and I made ready for flight,'' but the expected retreat never materializes. Confused and terrified, Basil then becomes a hero by saving the company's colors and killing many of the enemy by flailing about with the pole; indeed, when the Americans run away, Basil pursues them with a long pike, and many, he reports simply, ''shared the fate of Colin Frazer'' (249-50). Promoted to ensign, he sums up his heroic actions by saying, ''Never were any honours less deserved. I believe I did fight most furiously after I went fairly mad and had lost all sense of fear. . . . I had some confused notion that these Americans were all to be killed, and the

sooner we could get that done the better; and besides, I was in
great wrath at them, I suppose, for wanting to kill me" (251).
Such observations clearly anticipate modern protests against war's
confusion and absurdity.

If Basil seems a curious kind of hero, Clifford becomes the
complete antithesis of the typical heroine, even besides her unconventional name and background. Active, lively, independent, she
is one of Hogg's best characters. Her finest scene occurs when
Basil, fresh from his new honors, determines to continue his oft-
attempted project of marrying a rich woman, and meets Clifford
to cast her off. But Clifford, too, has a proposal and a confession:
"You must know," she tells Basil, "that there is scarce an officer
in your regiment who has not tried to seduce my affections from
you, and some of them have made me very tempting offers. I have
made a resolution, however, never to be either a mistress or wife
to any one in the same regiment with you, and under your eye;
but Major Ker of the dragoons has made me an offer that will
place me in affluence all the rest of my life. I am afraid that you
will weary of me, for I will become burdensome and expensive to
you, and your pay is small; and therefore I would not give him
any answer until I asked at you whether I should suffer myself to
be seduced by him or not." Basil accepts her story, but protests
that his friend Ensign Odogherty would not have been guilty of
such a discreditable act. "Bless your simple heart," she replies;
"Ensign Odogherty was the very first among them who made the
proposal, and what I refused to his blarney he was like to have
taken by force" (251). Overwhelmed by her loyalty and candor,
Basil reverses himself, and Clifford remains his mistress for
another three years, before marrying a wealthy old merchant,
bearing Basil's son, and living as a great lady.

The rest of Basil's story includes his accounts of further battles,
and his return to Scotland, where he witnesses some supernatural
occurrences on the Isle of Lewis, unrelated either to his theme or
to the narrative as a whole, and where he meets Clifford's father
in Inverness. The story ends with Basil's return to Edinburgh and
to his true occupation of trying to marry a rich woman. The final
episode parodies a fairy-tale ending when, as the last desperate
measure, Basil finally becomes engaged to a "worthy excellent
woman" with "gray eyes, shrivelled cheeks, a red nose, and a
considerable beard [which] moved with a kind of muscular

motion, like the whiskers of a cat. Though my stomach was like to turn at [her] display of the tender passion, I was obliged to ogle again, and press her to name a day, whereon I was to be made the happiest of men!'' (264). In the nick of time, however, Clifford, a rich widow, returns with their son; Basil can free himself, and they marry to begin a life ''so uniformly irregular, that the shortest memorandum . . . that I could draw up would be flat and unprofitable. . . . I am wearing down to the grave, sensible of having spent a long life of insignificance, productive of no rational happiness to myself, nor benefit to my fellow-creatures'' (265). In the last lines Basil restates the moral—''that without steadiness in a profession, success in life need not be expected; and without steadiness of principle we forego our happiness both here and hereafter''—and apologizes for his levity in dealing with female imprudence by saying that he was only adhering to the truth and that ''never yet was there a *young* female seduced from the paths of virtue, who did not grievously repent'' (265). As in *Moll Flanders*, the tale's life and animation, Basil's energy, Clifford's honesty, and the final reward—a rich wife—all belie the intended moral. Basil tells the truth only in offering his story as a source of amusement, for it stands as one of Hogg's most delightful burlesques.

Certainly the most famous of his comic pieces is ''The Witch of Fife.'' Though perhaps descended from Burns's ''Tam O' Shanter,'' one of the Shepherd's favorites, its chief elements—the earthy, pleasure-loving character of the hero, the exciting rides through the air to exotic places, the comic description and dialogue—all testify to Hogg's originality. Characteristically, the first half consists of a dialogue, in which an old man asks his wife where she has been; the wife's answer comes in long narratives, interrupted by mutterings of disbelief from her husband, of her travels with a group of witches, first to Lommond height, where they drank beer and danced till dawn, then to Norway, where they were washed with witch-water and slept with warlocks, and finally to Carlisle, where they broke into the bishop's wine-cellar and ''drank, and . . . drank of the bishopis wyne/Quhill we culde drynk ne mair.''

The old man listens, alternately flyting with and insulting his wife. When she tells of her changed beauty, he crows,

> Ye lee, ye lee, ye ill womyne,
>    Se loud as I heir ye lee!
> For the warst-faurd wyfe on the shoris of Fyfe
>    Is cumlye comparit wi' thee.

But for all his supposed concern for her desertion, he takes her
amorous dancing and dallying without becoming upset. The
bishop's wine, however, is another matter entirely, for he vows to
join them on their next flight to Carlisle "To drynk of the blude-
red wyne." And though his wife warns of the danger involved, he
nevertheless waits and finally catches them at a tryst. The poem,
now in the third person, tells of his great carouse as

> He dancit on the mouldy ground,
> And he sang the bonniest sangs of Fyfe,
> And he tuzzlit the kerlyngs round.

> And aye he piercit the tither butt,
>    And he suckit, and he suckit se lang,
> Quhill his een they closit, and his voice grew low,
>    And his tongue wald hardly gang.

Unfortunately, though, the witches leave without him, and the
guards who find him ask him to explain his presence; his head
spinning, he can only cry, "I cam fra Fyfe, . . ./And I cam on the
mydnycht wynde." They are about to burn him, when his wife
returns as a giant bird and whispers a magic word which enables
him to gleefully fly away:

> His armis war spred, and his heid was hiche,
>    And his feite stack out behynde;
> And the laibies of the auld manis cote
>    War wauffling in the wynde.

The English watch the two disappear, hearing only the old man's
laugh floating on the wind "With a lang and a loud gaffa."
   In this lively story with its brilliantly absurd but all-too-human
old man, Hogg burlesques many of the ballad techniques. Douglas
Mack calls the language "a kind of pseudo-antique Scots, clearly
an imitation of the Middle Scots of the old Makars. . . . Hogg
gives his language an air of antiquity mainly by means of spelling

—*quh-* for *wh-*, *-it* for *-ed*, and so on [without reproducing] Middle Scots accurately [although here] it provides an appropriate vehicle for the outlandish absurdities."[3] In addition to the ballad stanza, Hogg incorporates conventional epithets and repetitions, such as the "blude-red wyne" and "the auld guidman was ane cunnyng auld man,/And ane cunnyng auld man was he." Finally, Hogg proposes two moral lessons, but undercuts the first and makes the second as tongue-in-cheek as the conclusion of Burns's poem. About to be burned, the old man blames "all the ill wemyng/That lead puir men astray!" and laments his greedy desire to "Rin post to the deil for wyne." The wife's return and the old man's laughter mock both this moral and the Englishmen. The narrator admonishes every man of Fife to heed what drinkers endure, "And never curse his puir auld wife,/Rychte wicked altho scho be" (*Poems*, 13-16). Though this moral reverses the old man's mistaken judgment on his wife, it makes no comment on his greed or drunkenness. Nor should it, for such comic creations stand above moral censure.

Hogg acknowledged "The Witch of Fife" as "the most happy and splendid piece of humorous ballad poetry which I ever wrote," and gave credit to Scott for advice on changing the original ending wherein the old man was burned "skin and bone." Hogg recalls Scott as saying, "There never was such a thing written for genuine and ludicrous humour but . . . what had the poor old carl done to deserve such a fate? Only taken a drappy o' drink too much at another man's expense which you and I have done often. It is a *finale* which I cannot bear and you *must* . . . by some means or other no matter how extravagant or ridiculous . . . bring off the fine old fellow." Hogg then relates how he "certainly brought off the old man with flying colours which is by far the best part of the ballad" (*FA*, 123-24). But the whole piece testifies to Hogg's brilliant comic exaggeration.

## II  *Social Satire*

Burlesque enters into so many of Hogg's writings that it seems more a method than a type. Sir Simon Brodie and the old man of "The Witch of Fife" certainly have no serious intent: Sir Simon does not represent the Royalists, nor the goodman the Scots peasant. But when the burlesque has a point, satire results, and

Hogg, though usually neither bitter nor profound in his satire, nevertheless hits out at important targets, most commonly religious extremism, contemporary manners, and the literary world.

Religious concerns are evident in many of Hogg's writings. The moral tales warn against straying from the paths of virtue, and the *Lay Sermons* restates orthodox religious doctrines in simple terms. Since Hogg held basic and uncomplicated religious beliefs, he gives no consideration to deeper issues, just as in his historical tales. The tales of the Covenanters, the anecdotes of the '45, and Basil Lee's adventures in the American Revolution all use the historical setting without investigating the issues behind the historical events; instead, Hogg focuses on the human reactions and situations arising from those events. That Hogg is a Scots Tory *and* a Presbyterian peasant, hence with sympathies on both sides, explains his lack of interest in the political issues. Likewise, he deals with no theological issues, only with the misinterpretation or abuse of doctrine, itself never disputable as long as it is Christian rather than pagan, as in *Three Perils of Man* and *Queen Hynde*. In his religious satire Hogg treats the extremes of orthodox belief rather than sects or schisms. Writing from London, he noted: "I have this day been hearing the Rev. Edward Irving preach and lecture, and though I could not help being deeply affected by his eloquence, his sermon seemed the ravings of enthusiastic madness."[4] For Hogg, the enthusiasts and the hypocrites pose the great danger to the innocent and the zealot alike— after all, such misdirected excess led to the persecutions after Bothwell Bridge and Culloden.

The comic "Village of Balmaquhapple" illustrates the failings of both sinner and Pharisee. A prayer to St. Andrew for the salvation of a wicked town, the poem begins with a prologue:

> D'ye ken the big village of Balmaquhapple,
> The great muckle village of Balmaquhapple?
> 'Tis steep'd in iniquity up to the thrapple,
> An' what's to become o' poor Balmaquhapple?

The prayer proper gives a general catalogue of the town's sins, asking St. Andrew to

> save the great village of Balmaquhapple
> Frae drinking an' leeing, an' flyting an' swearing,
> An' sins that ye wad be affrontit at hearing,
> An' cheating an' stealing; oh, grant them redemption.

The charges then become more specific, directed at such hypocrites as

> Johnny the elder, wha hopes ne'er to need ye,
> Sae pawkie, sae holy, sae gruff, an' sae greedy;
> Wha prays every hour as the wayfarer passes,
> But aye at a hole where he watches the lasses.

Of Cappie the cobbler, Tammie the tinman, Dickie the brewer, Peter the skinman, Geordie the deacon, and Bess, "wha delights in the sins that beset her," the speaker exhorts:

> O worthy St. Andrew, we canna compel ye,
> But ye ken as weel as a body can tell ye,
> If these gang to heaven, we'll a' be sae shockit,
> Your garret o' blue will but thinly be stockit.

The narrator's complacency—like that of the townspeople of Mark Twain's Hadleyburg—and superiority toward the erring villagers has now surfaced, and that his nature differs little from the elder, for instance, can be seen in the final stanza:

> But for a' the rest, for the women's sake, save them,
> Their bodies at least, an' their sauls, if they have them; . . .
> An' save, without word of confession auricular,
> The clerk's bonny daughters, an' Bell in particular;
> For ye ken that their beauty's the pride an' the staple
> Of the great wicked village of Balmaquhapple!
>
> (*Poems*, 413)

More serious, because less exaggerated and more human, the unusual "First Sermon," with its tragic end and effective Wordsworthian blank verse, depicts a splendid but proud young clergyman. The narrator

> liked him not, he held his head so high;

> And ever and anon would sneer, and pooh!
> And cast his head all to one side, as if
> In perfect agony of low contempt
> At everything he heard, however just.
> Men like not this, and poets least of all.

Also, the narrator mocks the cleric's looks—red hair illustriously curled, narrow shoulders, and "a primming round the mouth, of odious cast,/Bespeaking the proud vacancy within." Nevertheless, he attends the young man's first sermon:

> Well, to the Old Greyfriars' Church I went,
> And many more with me. The place was crowded.
> In came the beadle—then our hero follow'd
> With gown blown like a mainsail, flowing on
> To right and left alternate; the sleek beaver,
> Down by his thigh keeping responsive time. . . .
> But I bethought me, what a messenger
> From the world's pattern of humility.

The face of "simpering seriousness" which seemed "A mockery of all things deem'd divine" pours forth the prayer, but impresses the listener only by its self-conceit. Then comes the sermon itself:

> O ye ruling Powers
> Of poesy sublime, give me to sing
> The splendours of that sermon! The bold *hem*!
> The look sublime that beam'd with confidence;
> The three wipes with the cambric handkerchief;
> The strut—the bob—and the impressive thump
> Upon the holy Book! No notes were there,
> No, not a scrap—All was intuitive. . . .

But then comes the grand horror, as the "grand and promised sermon" turns out to be a jumble of scraps from *Nature*, Johnson, Addison, Blair, Shakespeare, Young, and a host of poets and preachers; moreover, there is no plan or system, "no gleam of mind or aim—"

> A thing of shreds and patches—yet the blare
> Went on for fifteen minutes, haply more.
> The *hems*! and *haws*! began to come more close;

finally, his mind blank, the preacher stumbles out of the church. Then comes the strange, powerful ending, as the narrator says:

> how I admired
> The Scottish audience! There was neither laugh
> Nor titter; but a soften'd sorrow
> Portray'd in every face. As for myself,
> I laugh'd till I was sick; went home to dinner,
> Drank the poor preacher's health, and laugh'd again.
> But otherwise it fared with him; for he
> Went home to his own native kingdom—Fife,
> Pass'd to his father's stable—seized a pair
> Of strong plough-bridle reins, and hang'd himself.
>
> (*Poems*, 351-52)

The narrator concludes by suggesting that young beginners should have a written text, their own or another's, to read so as to ease the ordeal. The characteristic double satire becomes clear, though, since the minister's pride leads to his destruction, but the narrator reveals his own cynicism, his flippant religious attitudes, his lack of understanding of the tragedy in contrast with the audience's kindness, and, finally, his callousness. His final advice shows him concerned only with appearance, like the man he mocked.

If the young minister's failing comes from his conceit, however, the hypocritical John Clerk of *The Brownie of Bodsbeck* suffers from a more earthy passion. Importuned by Maron Linton, Laidlaw's wife, to save her daughter from supposed commerce with evil spirits, the curate suggests a novel form of exorcism: he will sit with Katharine all night in a locked room, "and with the help only of the Bible, the lamp, and the hour-glass, he declared that he would drive the unclean spirit from its tabernacle of clay." Moreover, he warns that if strange noises should be heard, "no one was to interfere, or even listen, upon pain of being delivered up to the foul spirit soul and body" (*Tales*, 32). Mass John then locks himself and Katharine in the Old Room and attempts to seduce her. Begging for time to reflect on his proposal, Katharine turns to her Bible; Mass John suggests some specific passages to consider, but she ignores him. When the sands of the hourglass run out—the time limit she had imposed—the curate lifts her and carries her to the bed, but suddenly a supposedly barred outer door opens, and a being of such unearthly dimensions entered, as no pen may ever wholly define. It was the Brownie of Bodsbeck, sometimes mentioned before, small of stature, and its whole form utterly misshaped. . . . [Mass John] sunk powerless on the floor, and, with a deep shivering groan, fainted away. Katharine, stretching forth her hands, flew to meet her unearthly guardian; "Welcome, my watchful and redoubted Brownie," said she, "thou art well worthy to be the familiar to an empress, rather than an insignificant country maiden."

> "Brownie's here, Brownie's there,
> Brownie's with thee everywhere,"

said the dwarfish spirit, and led her off in triumph.

(33)

The sudden appearance of the Brownie in the flesh, hitherto only a figure of rumor and superstition, astonishes the reader almost as much as Mass John.

The depraved curate, whom Katharine releases the next morning from the locked room, determines "to weather out the storm with as lofty and saintly a deportment as he could" (34). He claims some success in the exorcism and flatters the mother's "high and pure notions of religion, as well as her piety and benevolence" (42). He agrees again to protect the family, but Maron, to his dismay, leads him to the Old Room; later, old Nanny peeps in to see "four or five figures standing at the bed, resembling human figures in some small degree. . . . In the midst of them stood the deformed little Brownie [and] in his right hand he brandished a weapon, resembling a dirk or carving-knife." The Brownie accuses Mass John of being "a stain to thy profession, and a blot upon the cheek of nature, enough to make thy race and thy nation stink in the nose of their Creator" (42). In the morning, the goodwife finds Nanny delirious in the kitchen and no one at all in the Old Room. The curate is never again seen in the area, though Hogg does report a meeting between him and Clavers three years later in which the general declines to further the man's schemes of vengeance. The unrepentant and hypocritical clergyman makes but a brief appearance in the tale, but one that shows the church as not immune from human flaws. Those who depend on it uncritically, like Maron Linton, run tremendous risks for such blind confidence, whereas Katharine's innocence and virtue prove a greater defense against evil than her mother's trust in a man supposedly good because of the cloth he wears.

Hogg's best portrait of religious extremism, of course, occurs in the *Confessions* in the portraits of the deluded son and Pharisee father, the two Wringhims.

Perhaps less serious than his religious satire, but equally consistent, is Hogg's criticism of city manners. With his background of rural simplicity and common sense, Hogg distrusts the sophistication and affectation of most city folk, such people as the narrator of "The First Sermon," and without doubt men like Lockhart and Wilson and others of the *Blackwood's* group. These criticisms begin in *The Spy*, where, without qualifications, Hogg undertakes to survey "the taste and genius of his countrymen" (*Spy*, 4). And though some of Hogg's comments on the theater, the manners, and even the conduct of his own magazine seem superficial, most smack of country wisdom. All, however, rail against affectation. A letter in No. 7, for instance, castigates the conversation of literary parties as being "most insipid and dull, every individual appearing as if under some restraint" (49). An article against excess of singularity in No. 39 suggests that "in moral and religious questions only, a wise man will hold no consultation with fashion, because these duties are constant and immutable, and depend not on the notions of men, but the commands of Heaven" (308). In No. 7, also, appears the complaint of Fanny Lively, a young beauty "with the form and air of a Diana" and a voice like a nightingale, who knows "perfectly well that I was made intentionally to please the gentlemen," yet must leave the table with the other women and wait until later for the men, by then often drunk, to come in. Why do they say things, she asks with country simplicity, in the presence of God that they won't say before a young girl? Why are female conversations boring and male ones unrefined? She pleads with the Spy "to open the people's eyes to the propriety of mixed companies" (52). The Spy answers that although her proposal seems like a strategem to stay with the men, there seems no reason why "custom should persist in shutting up the most lovely and graceful part of the company" (55). In "Satirical Directions to Every Class in Edinburgh, in what manner to keep the Sabbath," the Spy chooses a Swiftian approach in offering "a few *serious* suggestions" (241). He advises gentlemen to lie long in bed, skip morning devotions, write letters, and only attend church two or three times a season, since a gentleman can do without God, and everlasting life is of no account. He counsels young gents to sleep long, worship in a mirror, read an amusing book, and attend a sermon only when fashionable young ladies are in attendance. Women, the Spy concludes, need no advice because they are already well trained in adorning their forms, the only thing necessary for them. These criticisms recur a decade later when Gatty Bell visits Edinburgh in *The Three Perils of Woman* and writes home about the wayward girls, the bad theater, the fashion of concealing true sentiments, and the lack of religion displayed by everyone but ladies and ministers (*3PW*, I, 103-104).

Of course the chief charge against the sophisticated city blades is their immorality. Hogg's seduced maidens usually hail from the country, whereas their lovers come from large estates and flee to the city. The peasant girl has traditionally had little defense against the educated wiles of such seducers except for her usual quick wit and clear sense of reality. The most readable part of all Hogg's plays, the second act of "The Bush aboon Traquair," a *jeu* slightly reminiscent of Burns's "Jolly Beggars," illustrates such a threat, in burlesque, with the foppish Pompey taking liberties with his mother's three servant girls, Ann, Mary, and Girzy. The girls have been discussing Ann's concept of fun: making fools of men and exposing their pretensions. Ann tells Mary, "Since we cannot make men as we would have them, what can a sensible maiden do but take them as they are. If we stand up, taking offense at every trifle, and every habitual failing, we may sit out our summer day, and be drafted off for eild crock ewes in the back year."[5] Upon Pompey's arrival, the baiting begins:

*Pomp.* Fine day, girls—fine day for pretty blooming maids—makes them blush like roses—Eh! does it not, Maria? . . .

*Mary.* It is your effrontery that makes us blush, sir! Keep your fingers to yourself, if you please.

*Pomp.* Always in the same humour, Maria! Wh— wh— why won't you allow a gentleman student just come from college a little toying?

*Mary.* Pray, sir, what may your studies at college be? Keep your distance if you please, meantime.

*Pomp.* Why, sweet Maria, I am at present studying municipal law.

*Mary.* I thought it could not be *civil* law—keep off! and take that as a lesson in meadow law (*striking him with her rake.*)

Mary and Girzy leave, and Pompey asks Ann if she has thought about his proposal; "Indeed I have, sir," she replies. "I have thought of nothing else, and am quite delighted, but am afraid our marriage—"

> *Pomp.* Our what? Marriage? Oh, my dear girl, don't name such a thing as that—quite a horrible concern!—stale beyond all sufferance!—No, no, it is not for that miserable creature a wife, that I want you; I love you far too much for that—I want you for my mistress.
>
> *Ann.* Alack, dear sir! I cannot hire you into my service, for I have no money to give you for wages, and no work for you. But I am willing to be your servant, or your wife; would not that be better, since you love me so?
>
> *Pomp.* No, no, no. I tell you no. I don't court you for marriage. I tell you I hate it—it is love only that I want—I cannot make you comprehend it. —Did you never hear of a dear, sweet thing called seduction?
>
> *Ann.* Seduction? O, that must be a grand thing! I should like it exceedingly. Is that one of the fine arts you learn at college?
>
> *Pomp.* Yes, charming innocent! It is the sweetest and the highest of all arts. I'll teach it you. (300-301)

Pompey's lessons, however, are interrupted by his mother, pleased to find him instructing her servants in "first principles." The Goodwife asks, "What is this blessed art called? Is it the doctrine of the Fall?" And Ann answers, "I suppose it is. . . . It is called I think seduction"; and after Pompey protests, she goes on, "You called it so to me, after you asked me to be your mistress you know, and I refused. It *is* something *duction*, *se*duction, or *pro*-duction. I am sure it was the one or the other" (304). The comedy may be broad, but Hogg's fears about the follies of education and idleness show more clearly and entertainingly here than in his moral tales.

Politics was for Hogg another constant, like religion and morals, in which the ideals—Tory ideals—were so clear that one need never deal with issues which could hardly be controversial to a man of common sense. Another exercise in Swiftian irony is occasioned by the Reform Bill, but Hogg ignores the politics in favor of a treatment of the controversy's effect on the people. The Shepherd admits, "I'm a Tory, and have been one since ever I can mind, which is now nearly three quarters of a century, but why or wherefore I should have been one is really more than I can tell

you. People's principles seem to be born with them, for, God
knows, I never had any interest in being a Tory. But, in these
letters, I shall let you see that I am neither Whig, Tory, Radical,
nor Destructionist, but merely a sincere lover of his country, and
an admirer of his countrymen, with all their ridiculous extrava-
gancies."[6] Then in four brief letters, Hogg supports the Reform
Bill because its discussion has already improved the conversation
and increased the amount of drinking. In addition, it makes
everyone a politician and brings easy fame; it also makes moral
discrimination easier, since honesty is defined by what party one
belongs to. Finally, perhaps most of all it benefits women by
interesting them in politics and thus keeping them "from reading
plays and romances, which are but too apt to inspire them with
wild and fanciful ideas"; indeed, "all the trumpery of novel
reading is given up for the pure and earnest flame of patriotism,"
and women look better when so animated. The fifth letter gives
up the satiric manner, though, and becomes a straightforward and
honest plea for tolerance. His original pose does not differ from
his true feelings, since tolerance and moderation are at the heart
of the Shepherd's political and religious ideas. Although he mentions in passing a fear of power-hungry mobs, Hogg treats the
issue as not one to be explored in depth, nor indeed one in which
he evinces much interest.

Hogg does note one other aspect of modern life which interests
him greatly: business. He could hardly avoid the commercial side
of life, living as he did in continual want of money, seeing himself
and his publishers go bankrupt time after time, and watching
fortunes being made and lost in this period of great money
dealings which preceded the even more incredible affairs of the
Victorian age. Though always in financial difficulties—his letters
usually set forth his bleak situation or ask for advances and
loans—he could still comment comically on the growing commercialism, especially if it threatened to ruin his beloved Scottish
scenery. In "Malise's Tour," Hogg notes the changes that have
taken place near Loch Katrine, the scene of *Lady of the Lake*.
Led by Highland guides who object to the poem's inaccuracies,
Hogg finds the tourist trade in full operation. Plans are underway
to have a ferry, piloted by a beautiful girl in tartans, take visitors
to the island home of Scott's heroine; another Highlander dresses
as a Goblin and skulks around the woods to impress the literary

pilgrims. At one point the narrator looks out over one of the famous views, but undercuts the literary sentimentalism by suggesting how much better it would look with a bottle of Scotch whisky for a companion.

Hogg's clearest opinions of modern business occur in a comic song curiously titled "March of Intellect," wherein the Shepherd paints a picture of speculation that would become even more real in the coming decades. The poet sings:

> Then fye let us a' to subscribing,
>   Since siller is no worth a plack,
> And the pence in the kist that lay mouling,
>   Will be turned into pounds in a crack!
> With our scheming, and steaming, and dreaming,
>   Can no cash-burdened Joint-stock be found
> To fill the auld moon wi' whale blubber,
>   And light her up a' the year round?

The increase in crime and confusion sounds modern, since "thieves will be nabb'd by the thousand,/And houses insured by the street." Noting that even courting will be done by steam, Hogg concludes:

> Then fye let us a' to subscribing,
>   And build up a tower to the moon. . . .
> Let's see a' how proud we can be,
> And build ower a brig to Kirkcaldy,
>   And drown a' the French in the sea!

> (*Poems*, 437)

Here Hogg equates "intellect" with useless "progress," perhaps because of his oft-cited contention that college provides useless education. Nor does it seem likely that his opinion of progress and commercialism would be changed by such modern proposals as a tunnel under the English Channel or the fact of a souvenir shop on his beloved St. Mary's Loch.

### III  *Literary Satire and Parody*

The one aspect of contemporary life that involved Hogg most—the literary—forms the basis for many satires. Yet here too the

Shepherd remained an outsider because of his age and back-ground; acquainted with, and victimized by, the younger writers and publishers who made Edinburgh a literary capital second only to London—Lockhart, Wilson, Maginn, Blackwood, and Con-stable—Hogg wrote several satires which have particular reference to Edinburgh literary personalities and quarrels. The most notorious of these writings, the "Chaldee MS.," appeared in the first number of the newly christened *Blackwood's* and caused such a sensation as to require Lockhart and Wilson to seek refuges in the country, to force Hogg to remain at home in Altrive, and to involve the publisher in lawsuits which included an out-of-court settlement for slander. The article, subsequently removed from bound volumes of the magazine, served its purpose well: ten thousand copies of the issue were sold, and the journal was established with a reputation for controversy and liveliness.

The original idea was Hogg's; he wrote an allegorical treatment in biblical style of the quarrel between Blackwood and his first editors, who had left to work for his arch-rival Constable. Dealing completely in personalities, the satire shows the opponents choosing sides for an Apocalyptic battle. The description of Blackwood, whose publishing house stood at 17 Princes Street, gives some indication of the style:

3. And I looked, and behold a man clothed in plain apparel stood in the door of his house; and I saw his name, and the number of his name; and his name was as it had been the colour of ebony, and his number was the number of a maiden, when the days of the years of her virginity have expired.

Constable appears thus in Hogg's original:

And in those days and at that time there lived also a man that was *crafty* in counsel and cunning in all manner of working; and the man was an upright and a just man, one who feared God and eschewed evil; and he never was accused before any judge of fraud, or of perjury, or of deceit; for the man was honourable among the sons of men.

Scott, "the great magician who dwelleth in the old fastness, hard by the river Jordan, which is by the Border," promises to remain neutral, and the two men gather together all the beasts to aid them, including "the great wild boar" (Hogg) and the scorpion

(Lockhart); before the final battle, however, the piece ends, as "I heard a great tumult, but I wist not what it was."[7]

Hogg's tolerance appears in the description of Constable, and it seems incredible that this relatively mild piece should cause such a stir. But Lockhart and Wilson expanded Hogg's idea during a long night fortified by punch. Some measure of their changes can be seen in the picture of Constable, for in the final version the verse stops after the first semicolon, leaving out Hogg's points about honesty and piety. In fact, the two editors doubled the length of the article, adding most if not all of the most scurrilous attacks at the end; Hogg, then, seems innocent of all but the original idea. Today, though, the piece still seems tame, especially in comparison with some of the brutal reviews which later appeared in *Blackwood's*, including several directed at the Shepherd himself, as well as the famous one of John Keats's *Endymion*. Hogg's more temperate treatment of his opponents occurs in "The Blue and the Yellow," a song mocking the Whig *Edinburgh Review* with its colored covers:

> If e'er you would be a brave fellow, young man,
> Beware of the Blue and the Yellow, young man;
> If ye wad be strang,
> And wish to write lang,
> Come join wi' the lads that get mellow, young man.
>
> (*Poems*, 431)

Only in some of his letters, written in deep anger and repented soon after, does Hogg exhibit anything like the Scorpion's sting.[8]

Hogg's comic commentary on literary affairs had begun much earlier with "Mr. Shuffleton's Allegorical Survey of the Scottish Poets of the Present Day," a three-part essay in *The Spy* wherein Mr. Shuffleton brings forth female puppets representative of contemporary poets, in the manner of Thackeray's *Vanity Fair*. Naturally, Scott receives the most praise for his "easy, rapid flow of the poetry, and in the simple and natural descriptions both of scenery and characters," though he is chided for unconnected tales and for a dearth of Scottish heroes (*Spy*, 76-77). Hogg's self-portrait is of most interest because of its recognition of the characteristics which others would later comment on. The girl first appears in an elegant dress (resembling Scott's and Campbell's), but with the ornaments disarranged; then she throws off her

encumbering mantle to appear "in the dress of a native shep-
herdess." She sweetly sings many of her native airs, but the crowd
criticizes her negligent dress. She is "a self-willed imp," according
to Mr. Shuffleton, "who thinks more of her accomplishments
than any other body does; and, because her taste is natural, thinks
it infallible, and every person wrong who does not acquiesce in
her opinion." When the Spy talks to her, she replies, "I think I
sude ken as weel as you, or ony like ye, what suits my ain form
an' features." And she departs in disgust, saying to her dog,
"Come away, my poor fellow; you an' me disna mak a good
appearance amang a' these pridefu' fock."[9] Gentle fooling was
Hogg's stock in trade, and if he used his contemporaries as
targets, he was careful never to overlook his own follies, a method
as evident in his satires as in his other works.

Certainly the comic writings which best show off his gentleness,
his mimicry, his variety, and his literary knowledge, are the
parodies which form *The Poetic Mirror*, the only book other than
the *Confessions* reprinted in the first half of the twentieth century.
Hogg's proposed anthology of poems by major poets appeared
instead as an anonymous collection of poems, one each purportedly by Byron and Hogg; two by Scott, Coleridge, and
Southey; and three by Wordsworth and Wilson. The "Author's
Advertisement" disclaims any merit other than having procured
the poems, and tells how most of the contributors entered
cordially into the project; "the pages which follow," he concludes, "will show how well they have kept their word" (*Poems*,
145). Hogg's ingenious parodies perfectly imitate the style and
exaggerate the content of the originals to achieve their effect; they
also stand alone as interesting works. This last point, so often
overlooked, remains one of the great achievements of Hogg's
volume. A few examples from his treatments of the better-known
poets will suffice to show Hogg's gift for parody.

First comes Byron's "The Guerilla," a blood-and-thunder
romance in Spenserian stanzas told by a disillusioned narrator:

> Sore for the selfishness of men I wail—
> Scarce other motives human action guide;
> And sore I pity those of intellect frail,
> Who in aught else save their own strength confide.
> That might, that soul, with heaven alone allied,
> May all the casual gusts of fate defy.

The story concerns the dark-haired, dark-eyed Alayni, who pursues Marot, the kidnaper of his beloved Kela; Alayni finds them too late, for Kela has been ruined. After killing Marot, Alayni turns on Kela, now "lost beyond recovering," and slays her as well. Then he makes a cross of blood on his breast, takes a lock of Kela's hair for his plume, and sets off to avenge himself on women:

> Blood was his joy, and havoc was his meed,
> His direful rage no living foe might shun;
> If there was bloody work or ruthless deed,
> Forthwith by him that bloody work was done.

Finally Alayni determines to sacrifice his women prisoners on a pyre, but, when opposed, the madman slips away, only to return that night and kill each woman individually. In the morning, "What horrors brain of wakening lover seared,/When in his arms he found the gelid clay,/Or rolled from his embrace the severed head away!" Alayni escapes, to carry on his bloody work, "Laughing aloud, yet pressing to his breast/A tiar of raven hair which every morn he kissed." Hogg enters into the spirit so much as to write a stanza of Byronic irony far removed from his own belief in God's supremacy:

> Millions have bled that sycophants may rule,
> Have fallen to dust and left no trace behind;
> And yet we say that Heaven is merciful,
> And loves and cares for all the human kind;
> And we will spread our hands, and mouthe the wind,
> With fulsome thanks for all its tenderness.
> Ah me! that man, preposterously blind,
> Should feel, hear, see, reflect, yet not the less
> Hope in his hopeless state of abject nothingness.
>
> (145-49)

From Byronic excess, Hogg shifts to the gentler romances of Scott and the mysterious ones of Coleridge in "Wat o' the Cleuch" and "Isabelle." The former, in three cantos, details the adventures of the young knight of the title who appears

                    on his berry-black steed,
Caparisoned, belted for warrior deed.
Oh, bold was the bearing, and brisk the career,
And broad was the cuirass, and long was the spear,
And tall was the plume that waved over the brow
Of that dark reckless borderer, Wat o' the Cleuch.

Wat travels to the Border abbeys, gaining help from one abbot,
disguising himself and his men as monks to capture traitors at
Kelso, and finally capturing the castle of Roxburgh in a fine
pitched battle. Scott's descriptive catalogues become, in Canto
One, a list of the forage which the monks obtain for Wat:

                Some came with bread, and some with ale,
                Some came with butter, cheese, and kail,
                And some with doughty cogs of brose,
                The dole and dread of Scotland's foes!
                And—gladsome sight to warrior's eye—
                Came in the haggis, reeking high
                In fair and full rotundity.
                The bull-trout, pike, and grayling blue,
                The salmon of the silvery hue,
                With wood-cock, plover, and curlew; . . .
                Such only may and will I note,
                As suiteth rhythm, and rhyme and rote.
                                                    (154)

Another eighteen lines follow, listing more victuals which are,
however, consumed in the space of just eight lines.

   Hogg's less successful treatment of Coleridge emphasizes the
poet's wandering attempts to specify the subjective observations
of nature, as the heroine prepares to face some ghosts:

                It is a strange and lovely night,
                A grayish pale, but not white!
                Is it rain, or is it dew,
                That falls so thick I see its hue?
                In rays it follows, one, two, three,
                Down the air so merrily,
                Said Isabelle; so let it be!

Hogg exaggerates Coleridge's numerical preoccupations in the lines

> There are three times three, and three to these,
> Count as you will, by twos or threes;
> Three for the gallows, and three for the wave,
> Three to roast behind the stone,
> And three that shall never see the grave. . . .
>
> (175-76)

The Coleridge pieces lack story, and with Hogg's narrative imagination not being called into play, he can only exaggerate an uninteresting style.

The greatest parodies, however, consist of three portions of "The Recluse, A Poem," in which Hogg presents Wordsworth at his most self-consciously poetic. "The Stranger" is a non-tale of an uncouth rider who meets a boy

> With basket on his arm—and it appeared
> That there was butter there, for the white cloth,
> That over it was spread, not unobserved,
> In tiny ridges gently rose and fell,
> Like graves of children covered o'er with snow.

The boy agrees to hold the stranger's horse awhile, thinking of using the anticipated tip to buy some cakes, but

> Long, long he patient stood: the day was hot,
> The butter ran in streamlets, and the flies
> Came round in thousands—o'er the horse's head
> A moving, darkening canopy they hung,
> Like the first foldings of the thunder-cloud
> That, gathering, hangs on Bowfell's hoary peak.

The stranger does not return, and the horse becomes more restless as a storm approaches; Hogg juxtaposes levels of language nicely when he writes that the angry steed

> Turned round his head with such precipitance
> To dash the insects from his glossy side,
> That the poor boy in veriest danger stood
> To have his brains knocked out.

After noting the boy's amazement at the horse's motions—"for on similitude/In dissimilitude, man's sole delight/And all the sexual intercourse of things,/Do most supremely hang"—the poet reveals that, the stranger never returning, the boy goes home, his hand sunburned and his "basket, butter, cloth/. . . all one piece coherent."

The scene then shifts to a recent meeting with other poets: Southey ("The changeful and right feeble bard now styled/The Laureate"), Wilson ("of the Palmy Isle,/The man of plagues, horrors, and miseries"), Hogg ("In dialect most uncouth and language rude"), and Scott ("The Border minstrel—he of all the world/Farthest from genius or from common sense./He too, the royal tool"—this latter jibe suggesting indeed Hogg's displeasure over Scott's refusal to contribute). This group finds in the lake the skeleton of the stranger which proves the boy's strange story true; the narrator recounts the poets' reactions:

> It boots not here to tell all that was said.
> The laureate, sighing, uttered some few words
> Of most sublime and solemn tendency.
> The shepherd spoke most incoherent stuff
> About the bones of sheep, that on the hills
> Perish unseen, holding their stations so.
> And he, the man of palms, said nothing meet.

The relative silence gives the Wordsworthian narrator the chance to expatiate on "Regenerative Nature," "the thinking, thoughtless school-boy," "the soul sublimed and pure," "the fluctuation, and decay of things," and the "aim and end of prescient reason," in some forty lines. After noting how the others are "thunderstruck," the poet continues, but suddenly spies, approaching the skeleton, an ominous form whose shape

> Was like a coffin, and its colour such,
> Black as the death-pall or the cloud of night.
> At sight of such a hideous messenger,
> Thus journeying through the bowels of the deep,
> O'er sluggish leaf and unelaborate stone,
> All nature stood in mute astonishment,
> As if her pulse lay still. Onward it came. . . .
> I saw it shake its hideous form, and move

Towards my feet—the elements were hushed,
The birds forsook their singing, for the sight
Was fraught with wonder and astonishment.
It was a tadpole—somewhere by itself
The creature had been left, and there had come
Most timeously, by Providence sent forth,
To close this solemn and momentous tale.

(163-66)

Hogg writes that "had the imitations of Wordsworth been less a
caricature, the work might have passed, for a season at least, as
the genuine productions of the authors themselves" (*Mem*, 39).
Certainly the parodies are unrestrained, yet they contain nothing
scurrilous.

Never loath to leave himself out of a gathering of great poets,
as in "The Stranger," Hogg includes a self-parody, "The Gude
Greye Katt," as, he says, "a caricature of 'The Pilgrims of the
Sun,' the 'Witch of Fife,' and some others of my fairy ballads. It
is greatly superior to any of them" (*Mem*, 39). Though in no way
superior, the ballad contains most of the elements of Hogg's
narratives, and in none too exaggerated a form. The story describes an exotic journey through the air, the punishment of the
wicked, and the disappearance of innocent girls to another world;
typical characters include the Queen of Fairy Land, a wicked
churchman, seven beautiful heroines, and a Christian father;
and the themes concern the virtuous education of women, the
equation of fairy spirits with good, and even a final moral. Yet
many of his other poems exaggerate these elements as well, in
both comic and serious terms. The only real parody is in the
language and form itself, for Hogg intensifies the pseudomedieval
dialect and the ballad repetition so much as to make the poem
almost unreadable, as the first two stanzas illustrate:

There wase ane katt, and ane gude greye katt,
    That duallit in the touir of Blain;
And mony haif hearit of that gude katt,
    That neuir shall heare agayn.

Scho had ane brynd upon her backe,
    And ane brent abone hir bree;
Hir culoris war the merilit heuis
    That dappil the krene berrye.

(172-75)

Hogg later "translated" the poem (as he did others with pseudo-antique spelling), and as a straight comic piece it stands among his best with its balladlike simplicity.

Hogg's comic spirit, then, is a gentle one, partaking of burlesque and occasional bawdiness, but never of bitterness and rarely of biting attack. If his satiric targets were relatively easy ones—religious hypocrites, citified gallants, Byronic excesses, Wordsworthian banality—there can be little question of the effectiveness with which he did hit them. The final test of humor, after all, is how long it survives, and Hogg's comic flights, as the above examples illustrate, have much modern appeal, especially in their own good-natured excesses. Hogg's talent for pure comedy—entertaining humor—is documented by his works and by contemporary accounts; it was an easy task for the amiable Shepherd. Far more difficult, in ages of rationalism, is making people believe in the supernatural. It was a problem Hogg faced in his own time, and one which his works still face today. That he could present the supernatural effectively perhaps remains his greatest achievement, the one which substantiates his claim to be "king o' the mountain an' fairy school" of literature (*FA*, 118).

## CHAPTER 6

# *Fairies and Fiends*

"**W**ITHOUT something a little tinged with the supernatural," Hogg writes, "a tale has few charms for me."[1] Even more than history and humor, the supernatural and the horrific pervade his poetry and prose. Hogg is usually at his best with it because of both his deep understanding of the way extraordinary occurrences can affect the human mind and his ability to communicate these reactions effectively by drawing on all the narrative devices at his command. In his supernatural pieces, too, Hogg often presents more significant themes, as he deals with problems of appearance and abnormal psychology not found in his purely moralistic or entertaining works. The *Confessions*, *The Pilgrims of the Sun*, *The Brownie of Bodsbeck*, "The Brownie of the Black Haggs," and a handful of shorter tales and poems testify to the variety and brilliance of Hogg's almost unmatched genius in this field.

## I *Hogg and Superstition*

The chief reason for the effectiveness of the supernatural in Hogg's works is his own ambivalent attitude. Having grown up not only with faery ballads but with his family traditions—his grandfather, of course, had spoken with the fairies—Hogg came to manhood among people with strong beliefs in the powers of supernatural beings. In the *Queen's Wake*, the Bard of Ettrick sings, "E'er since, in Ettrick's glens so green,/Spirits, though there, are seldom seen;/And fears of elf, and fairy raid,/Have like a morning dream decayed," and Hogg appends a footnote: "The fairies have now totally disappeared; and it is pity they should; for they seem to have been the most delightful little spirits that ever

125

haunted the Scottish dells. There are only very few now remaining alive who have ever seen them. . . . But, strange as it may appear, with the witches it is far otherwise. Never, in the most superstitious ages, was the existence of witches, or the influence of their diabolical power, more firmly believed in, than by the inhabitants of the mountains of Ettrick .Forest at the present day" (*Poems*, 24). Though Hogg became better read and better educated, he could never have completely forgotten his earlier beliefs, especially with reminders of ghostly things all about him, in tales, poems, and eyewitness accounts. In a note to *The Mountain Bard*, Hogg details several beliefs about bogles, ghosts, and other strange appearances, and concludes, "Many are apt to despise their poor illiterate countrymen for these weak and superstitious notions; but I am still of opinion, that in the circumstance of their attaching credit to them, there is as much to praise as to blame. Let it be considered, that their means of information have not been adequate to the removal of these; while on the other hand, they have been used to hear them related, and attested as truths, by the very persons whom they were bound to reverence and believe" (*Poems*, 64-65n.). Such a situation was Hogg's own. Later, in a letter to his brother written from Edinburgh, the citified Shepherd jokingly remarks about his servant, "I have the ugliest old woman at present whom perhaps you ever saw. I rather fear she is a witch."[2] If he never explicitly committed himself either way, he at least had such firsthand understanding that in his works, told typically from the country people's point of view, he could create the effect of belief.

A clear stance can be found in "Superstition," where Hogg admits that superstition has lost its power, but laments the fact in a curious way—equating that loss of belief with the loss of faith in general. Of Superstition, "a sovereign of supreme unearthly eye," who once reigned in Scotland, Hogg writes,

> No human power her potence could restrain,
> No human soul her influence deny:
> Sole empress o'er the mountain homes, that lie
> Far from the busy world's unceasing stir:
> But gone is her mysterious dignity,
> And true Devotion wanes away with her;
> While in loose garb appears Corruption's harbinger.

The absence of Superstition makes it difficult for the "visionary bard" to "sing of visions that have been,/And cherish hope of visions yet to be." Then Hogg catalogs the effects she had on simple minds, his own as well, concluding,

> Oh! I have bowed to her resistless sway, . . .
> The note of gloaming bee that journeyed by
> Sent through my heart a momentary knell;
> And sore I feared in bush or brake might lie
> Things of unearthly make—for I knew well,
> That hour with danger fraught more than when midnight fell.

His lament for past times of holiness, of fancy, of high poesy, grows until finally he cries, "I wish for these old times, and Stuarts back again" (*Poems*, 392-94).

The crucial point here is the relationship between belief in the supernatural and in religion—faith in both depends on acceptance of things unseen. Hogg sees no inconsistency in maintaining beliefs in both faery lore and Christianity; indeed, he often places the two in situations of equal opposition, as with the friar and the wizard in *Three Perils of Man*. "If every creed has its attendant ills," he writes in "Superstition," "How slight were thine!—a train of airy dreams!/No holy awe the cynic's bosom thrills;/Be mine the faith diverging to extremes!" Complete dependence upon reason, though, may have equally disastrous effects, since "This high belief in Providence's sway,/In the eye of reason wears into decline;/And soon that heavenly ray must ever cease to shine."

Moreover, as the Shepherd points out in this poem and illustrates in his tales, faery creatures are not necessarily malignant. Superstition "filled'st the guilty heart with dread,/And brought the deeds of darkness to the day!" Were the incantations, exorcisms, and magic rites sins, Hogg asks; "Ah! no—'twas all in fair defense of right" (*Poems*, 394). Indeed, most of the spirits in Hogg's works appear for some beneficial purpose—the Brownie of Bodsbeck, after all, saves the heroine, and most of the ghosts expose murders. Even evil spirits have their use in providing antagonists against whom to test one's faith. In "The Witches of Traquair," Hogg maintains that "there is no person who is so apt to overshoot his mark as the devil. He must be a great fool in the main; for, with all his supposed acuteness, he often runs himself into the most egregious blunders that ever the leader of an opposition got into the midst of. Throughout all the annals of the human race, it is manifest, that whenever he was aiming to do the most evil, he was uniformly employed in such a way as to bring about the most good" (*Tales,* 394).

In addition to showing the beneficent side of the supernatural, Hogg carefully differentiates among the various creatures he presents. Of course, the possibility always exists that the spirits can be explained away, but those creatures who clearly act on the lives of mortals reveal traits and motives appropriate to their forms. In "The Wool-Gatherer," the kindly servant Barnaby, leading the heroine to refuge at his parents' house, whiles away the time by telling some marvelous, brief ghost stories, and "the seriousness of Barnaby's manner made it evident to his fellow-traveller that he believed in the reality of every word he had said." He explains that "ye had need to tak care how ye dispute the existence of fairies, brownies, and apparitions [at my parents']; ye may as weel dispute the gospel o' Saint Matthew. We dinna believe in a' the gomral fantastic bogles an' spirits that fley light-headed fock up an' down the country, but we believe in a' the apparitions that warn o' death, that save life, an' that discover guilt." Barnaby then recites a catalog of supernatural beings, along with their spheres of influence: "The deil an' his agents, they fash nane but the gude fock, the Cameronians, an' the prayin ministers, an' sic like. Then the bogles, they are a better kind o' spirits; they meddle wi' nane but the guilty, the murderer, an' the mansworn, an' the cheater o' the widow an' fatherless; they do for *them.* Then the fairies, they're very harmless, they're keener o' fun and frolic than aught else; but if fock neglect kirk ordinances, they see after *them.* Then the brownies, he's a kind o' half-spirit half-man; he'll drudge an' do a' the wark about the town for his meat, but then he'll no work but when he likes for a' the king's dominions" (*Tales,* 70). And in "Tibby Johnston's Wraith," David Proudfoot explains the distinctions between wraiths: they "are of twa kinds, you see. They appear always immediately before death, or immediately after it. Now when a wraith is seen before death, that is a spirit sent to conduct the dying person to its new dwelling. . . . These are sometimes good, and sometimes bad spirits, just according to the tenor of the person's life that lies on the bed o' death. . . . Now, when the wraith appears after death, that's the soul o' the deceased, that gets liberty to appear to the ane of a' its acquaintances that is the soonest to follow it; and it does that just afore it leaves this world for the last time" (*Tales*, 188). These definitions show how most inhabitants of the faery world serve moral purposes. Such treatment of faery lore distinguishes Hogg's use of the supernatural from the attempt merely to terrify, as in popular Gothic fiction.

Hogg's supernatural beings also enable him to move from everyday reality without limiting his use of comic characters or descriptive scenery; he can show a world in which good and evil interact, and where things unseen have more importance and power than things observed. Hogg can reveal the workings of Providence in more ways than just the poetic justice of a denouement, by suggesting the invisible protectors of the innocent. Dreams, too, come to play increasingly significant roles in the stories; and the problem of disbelief leads to discussions of appearance and reality. And, finally, in showing the reactions of the characters to real or imagined supernatural events, Hogg moves into the realm of abnormal psychology, that world later to be explored by Poe using many of the same methods. Poe says, in *Tales of the Grotesque and Arabesque*, that "terror is not of Germany, but of the soul"; Hogg concludes "Superstition" by calling her "Great ruler of the soul, which none can rule like thee!"

## II  *Other Worlds*

Hogg often treats the supernatural through a journey to another world, sometimes in a dream but not always; in either case, the experience has a tremendous impact. In "George Dobson's Expedition to Hell," an Edinburgh hackney driver undertakes to drive an elderly gentleman and his son outside town, though he doesn't know the way. But the man replies, "There is no man in Scotland who knows the road to that place better than you do. You have never driven on any other road all your life" (*Tales*, 311). George takes them, his horses racing at an unnatural speed, until they pass a large gate and come to a dark, murky, undefined place where he hears "a rushing sound, like that of a town on fire" (312). He promises to return the next day at noon, and prepares to leave. After finding the gate, where he recognizes the assistant gatekeepers as two young lawyer friends, he is refused exit by a churlish guard; when he asserts himself, as a licensed cab-driver, the keeper informs him that he is in Hell. "This was rather a damper to George," but he signs a note to say he will return at noon, and sets off in pursuit of his runaway horses. He finds them terribly mangled, with his carriage in ruins, but then, abruptly, his wife wakes him from the extraordinary dream. However, she and a doctor cannot convince him that his equipage is whole, or that his noon engagement with Mr. R—— of L——y is not real. George shows the red marks of the porter's hands on his throat, develops a fever, and vows to fulfill his bond. Eventually "he turned his face towards the wall, groaned deeply, and fell into a lethargy. . . . George never spoke more, save calling to his horses, as if encouraging them to run with great speed; and thus in imagination driving at full career to keep his appointment, he went off in a paroxysm, after a terrible struggle, precisely within a few minutes of twelve o'clock" (314). The final paragraph adds more "facts" to the incident: on the night of the dream, a London ship sank in a hurricane, drowning Mr. R—— and his son; George could not have known of this event, nor of the deaths of the two lawyers the evening before. As usual in his most effective stories, Hogg adds no further explanation or speculation—it stands as a common report of a local incident.

Another kind of hell—this one based on specific horrible details—becomes the dream home of the shepherd-hero of "Connel of Dee," who longs for a beautiful wife and an easy life. He does meet a seemingly virtuous woman who marries him and takes him to her castle for "pleasures that never can fail." But these lush delights do pall, and Connel thinks himself "placed on the confines of hell." The guests turn into "a profligate breed,/ The scum of existence to vengeance decreed,/Who laughed at their God and their friend." His wife takes lovers, and when he complains, she takes him to the dungeon where she orders the head of a former husband to be cut off. Terrified, Connel rushes from the castle, pursued by the wife and her paramours, eludes them in a barren land, and finally plunges into the River Dee. Then Hogg describes, in excruciating detail, Connel's sensations after drowning:

> The minnow, with gushet sae gowden and braw,
> The siller-ribbed perch, and the indolent craw,

> And the ravenous ged, with his teeth like a saw,
> Came all on poor Connel to feed.

Worst of all are the eels, as

> Their slid slimy forms lay his bosom upon,
> His mouth that was ope, they came near;
> They guddled his loins, and they bored thro' his side,
> They warped all his bowels about on the tide.

Connel awakes on the hillside and realizes that all has been a dream, but he never loses his fears; he hides from galloping riders; he thinks his "wife" may spy him at market. Now satisfied with his country life, he no longer desires "the gay and voluptuous" world. He praises goodness, sings sweetly, and lives long; "He loved and he cherished each thing that had life,/With two small exceptions, an eel and a wife,/Whose commerce he dreaded the same" (*Poems*, 287-91). Connel, too, has his life changed by a dream, though in a comic not a tragic fashion.

Far from the hells of George Dobson and Connel lies the world of "Kilmeny." For all the attacks on the Shepherd by his so-called friends in *Blackwood's*, it is always "Kilmeny" that they come back to in praise. Though Wilson makes a typical comment, referring to *Three Perils of Man* as "like all his things—a mixture of the admirable, the execrable, and the tolerable," early in the *Noctes*, he later calls "Kilmeny" the "finest Pastoral Lyric in our tongue."[3] Although Hogg mentions in a footnote to "The Witch of Fife" that "Kilmeny" is set in Fairyland, Douglas Mack points out that it really concerns a Christian heaven;[4] the poem indeed affirms the conjunction of the faery and religious worlds indicated above. "That land to human spirits given," to which Kilmeny is taken, consists of "The lowermost vales of the storied heaven," from which can be seen both the world below and the sapphire-studded gates of heaven, "More glory yet unmeet to know." Written in four-beat rhymed couplets, with varying feet and occasional triplets and quatrains, and sung by a religious mystic in the *Queen's Wake*—thus truly harking back to medieval minstrelsy—"Kilmeny" tells how the purest maiden on earth disappears mysteriously, then returns to earth for a month and a day to recount the visions she has seen, before returning forever to the "land of thought."

The poem contrasts the peaceful, heavenly world with the sinful earthly one, and includes prophetic passages on Queen Mary and the Napoleonic wars. The lush descriptions of the unworldly landscapes, however, remain the most memorable parts, drawing as they do on ballad techniques of repetition and unearthliness. The bard sings that "Kilmeny had seen what she could not declare;/Kilmeny had been where the cock never crew,/Where the rain never fell, and the wind never blew." It is a land of love and light, but without sun or moon. Kilmeny's purity has brought her to the attention of the inhabitants, those spirits commissioned to watch womankind, "For it's they who nurse the immortal mind." They lead her away,

> And she walked in the light of a sunless day:
> The sky was a dome of crystal bright,
> The fountain of vision, and fountain of light:
> The emerant fields were of dazzling glow,
> And the flowers of everlasting blow.

The spirits wash her in a stream of life, giving her eternal youth and beauty; then they show her this "land of thought":

> She looked, and she saw nae land aright,
> But an endless whirl of glory and light:
> And radiant beings went and came
> Far swifter than wind, or the linked flame.

She sees, finally, a vision of Scotland marred by war and bloodshed, and, becoming homesick, she begs to return to tell the maidens what she has seen and to remind them "That all whose minds unmeled remain/Shall bloom in beauty when time is gane." Even on earth she retains her spiritual beauty, without pride or passion, her voice "like the distant melodye,/That floats along the twilight sea," as she wanders in the glens, far from the haunts of men, singing her hymns. The poem concludes with a biblical scene as the wild beasts gather about her and are tamed—"It was like an eve in a sinless world!" (*Poems*, 32-35). Hogg's world of thought is not, of course, an intellectual land, but rather a vague, idyllic place, full of sensuous beauty but with peace and mildness rather than life and passion the keynotes—it is truly the vision of the mystical Bard of Ern rather than of the Ettrick Shepherd, but no less lovely on that account.

Far more complex, indeed thematically the most ambitious of all his works, is *The Pilgrims of the Sun,* Hogg's four-part epic dedicated to Byron, "Not for thy crabbed state-creed, wayward wight,/Thy noble lineage, nor thy virtues high/ [but for] thy bold and native energy;/Thy soul that dares each bound to overfly." A compendium of Hogg's modes, the poem ranges from a tour of the solar system, with its Miltonic cosmology, to a Scottish ghost story with an evil monk and a reviving corpse. More importantly, it provides a clear insight into the Shepherd's views of religion and mankind. In brief, the poem follows the heroine, Mary Lee, of Kilmeny-like purity, taken from Scotland by a youth and flown to the sun, the throne of God, and from there to several planets before being returned home full of new visions and new wisdom to impart to her friends.

The first part, written in ballad form, introduces Mary, conventionally beautiful but atypically intellectual, for

> She learned to read, when she was young,
>   The books of deep divinity;
> And she thought by night, and she read by day,
>   Of the life that is, and the life to be.
>
> And the more she thought, and the more she read
>   Of the ways of Heaven and Nature's plan,
> She feared the half that the bedesmen said
>   Was neither true nor plain to man.
>
> (Poems, 127)

Growing weary of this world and anxious to see the next, she meets, on a magical night when the fairies and elves are abroad, a young man with angelic face who invites her to accompany him; she dons a white robe, rises away from her body, and speeds through the air toward the sun, her guide offering a prayer that indeed "proved that the half the bedesmen said/Was neither true nor ever could be" (128). They pass through space "where no attractive influence came;/There was no up, there was no down,/But all was space, and all the same";[5] soon they pass two green planets, the second one superior to the first, with mortals "in the bloom of youth" and "no grave in all the land,/Nor church, nor yet a church-yard stone" (129); finally, they reach their goal, the chambered sun, the throne of God.

Part Second, written in blank verse designed to imitate the Metrical Psalms, explains the First, for it sets forth the structure of the universe. Mary and Cela, the guide, observe "the motioned universe, that wheeled around/In fair confusion." Unhampered by clouds or haze, they look on

> all nature—all that was they saw;
> But neither moon, nor stars, nor firmament,
> Nor clefted galaxy was any more.
> Worlds beyond worlds, with intermundane voids
> That closed and opened as those worlds rolled on,
> Were all that claimed existence: each of these,
> From one particular point of the sun's orb,
> Seemed pendent by some ray or viewless cord,
> On which it twirled and swung with endless motion.
>                                                                 (130)

Viewing "the plan/Of God's fair universe," Mary finds the earth not "the fairest and the most material part/Of God's creation," but actually "a thing subordinate—a sphere/Unseemly and forbidding" though still connected to God with its golden cord. Mary then asks about these worlds:

>                                                     Have they all fallen,
> And sinned like us? And has a living God
> Bled in each one of all these peopled worlds?
> Or only on yon dank and dismal spot
> Hath one Redeemer suffered for them all?

Cela's answer is equivocal, but the basis of Hogg's conception:

> More thou shalt know hereafter; but meanwhile
> This truth conceive, that God must ever deal
> With men as men—those things by him decreed,
> Or compassed by permission, ever tend
> To draw his creatures, whom he loves, to goodness;
> For he is all benevolence, and knows
> That in the paths of virtue and of love
> Alone can final happiness be found.
>                                                                 (131)

Calvinist foreknowledge and the complete sovereignty of God, mixed with Deist perfectibility, form the structure of a universe of life modeled not on churchly hierarchy but on perfect harmony and love. Passing on through the outer heaven, Mary sees saints and martyrs of all creeds, features, and hues, and she reflects "on this strange mystery,/So ill conform[ed] to all she had been taught/From infancy to think, by holy men." She finds childish the idea "that the Almighty's love,/Life, and salvation could to single sect/Of creatures be confined." After scenes of lush beauty and song as they approach the great throne itself, the pilgrims see a comet, a world whose "time/That God ordained for its existence run" which has had its golden cord cut so that it must wander outcast through the universe while all creation weeps. "The time will come," says Cela, "when in like wise, the earth/Shall be cut off from God's fair universe;/Its end fulfilled" (134).

From the Israelite harp of Part Second, Hogg turns to the English heroic couplet—"thou old bass—I love thy lordly swell,/With Dryden's twang, and Pope's malicious knell"—for the third section, an investigation of the worlds themselves and of the nature of mankind. Cela explains the pattern of the universe: the progression of planets, each peopled by human spirits, is a progression of goodness;

> The globes from heaven which most at distance lie
> Are nurseries of life to these so nigh. . . .
>     Thus 'tis ordained—these grosser regions yield
> Souls, thick as blossoms of the vernal field,
> Which after death in relative degree,
> Fairer or darker as their minds may be,
> To other worlds are led, to learn and strive
> Till to perfection all at last arrive.
>
> (135)

Perfection thus exists in the planets closest to the sun—the green and *churchless* world—with the final goal the Godhead itself. The two worlds described in most detail are those of lovers and warriors. In the former, Cela excuses some of woman's failings, since "Proud haughty man, the nursling of her care,/Must more than half her crimes and errors bear," just as the gardener is more responsible for the flower's failure to bloom. The second "world of pride, of havoc, and of spleen" consists of soldiers rehearsing all the future wars of earth. Cela explains the need to establish the rule of right, though at great cost, for

> Over thy world in ages yet to be
> Must desolation spread and slavery,
> Till nations learn to know their estimate;
> To be unanimous is to be great:
> When right's own standard calmly is unfurled,
> The people are the sovereigns of the world.

If not quite Tennyson's "Federation of the world," Hogg at least sees the need for a similar kind of world harmony through which "Truth, love, and knowledge, must prevail at last" (137). Mary and Cela pass on to other worlds described only briefly: those of sailors; of bards and their maidens; of "bedesmen discontent"; of "snarling critics bent with aspect sour/T' applaud the great and circumvent the poor"; and, most accursed of all, a world of lawyers where "all the language was of mystic mood,/A jargon nor conceived nor understood/. . . of deeds, respondents, and replies,/Dark quibbles, forms, and condescendencies." Finally Mary learns and accepts the two laws of the universe: "Through nature's range thou see'st a God in all" and human life is but the infant stage/Of a progressive, endless pilgrimage/To woe, or state of bliss . . ./At that eternal fount where being sprung" (138). Cela returns Mary to earth, to the country graveyard of her ancestors.

For the final part, Hogg returns to his "ancient harp," four-beat couplets, to tell a fine ghost story. Her body found on the lea, Mary had been mourned and buried, but an evil monk, seeking the gold and jewels buried with her, opens the grave to rob it. Just as he prepares to cut off the fingers to obtain the rings, Mary's spirit returns to her body; she screams, and the monk runs off, insane, as Mary makes her way home with bleeding hand. With amazement on both sides, Mary learns of her death and burial, and her parents hear of her journey. Gradually she becomes accepted in the social world, though always with some suspicion; the churchmen attack her vision, for

> through all space it well was known,
> By moon or stars, the earth or sea,
> An up and down there needs must be.
> This error caught their minds in thrall;

> 'Twas dangerous and apocryphal,
> And this nice fraud unhinged all.
> So grievous is the dire mischance
> Of priestcraft and of ignorance.
>
> (141)

Dazzlingly beautiful, Mary refuses all offers of marriage until one day Hugo of Norway, a bard who resembles Cela, arrives singing a song from the heavenly world. Hugo, with no memory of his past, is only searching for one Mary Lee. They marry and live in the mountains, far from the Border wars, for "he loved not the field of foray and scathe,/Nor the bow, nor the shield, nor the sword of death." The poem turns allegorical as Hugo becomes

> The first who attuned the pastoral reed
> On the mountains of Ettrick, and braes of Tweed;
> The first who did to the land impart
> The shepherd's rich and peaceful art.
>
> (143)

*Pilgrims* never achieved the success which Hogg hoped for it, although his footnotes suggest some reactions against it from the clergy. Nevertheless, it presents his clear humanitarian and optimistic religious views. The poetic progression—using Scottish metrical forms for the opening and closing sections in his native land, Psalmic blank verse for the picture of God, and English heroic couplets for satirical commentary on man's nature—attempts to merge form and content, and also demonstrates competence in handling these forms, for, unlike the other long poems, little poor poetry occurs to mar the splendid visual and narrative effects. The fourth part, though a superb horror story, fails to complement the first three in elevation of theme or content, but then Hogg characteristically had difficulty ending his pieces. Another problem is the inconsistency of the cosmic view: the earth at one time is in a neglected corner of the universe, but later serves as an important way-station where all souls must either pass through to a better world or be sent back to a worse one on the basis of their earthly acts. The entire poem, however, remains a remarkable achievement, one central to Hogg's visionary works.

### III   *This Sinfu' World*

Even when describing various hells and heavens, however, Hogg always exhibits a deep concern for the affairs of this world. Most of his supernatural stories take place in a fairly recognizable Scotland, though one where faery creatures, another part of God's creation, appear as a natural occurrence. Usually these beings serve as agents of good rather than of evil, though whether they are truly supernatural or rationally explicable seems to have little significance, since only the results are important. Often the stories, like "Adam Bell," leave many unanswered questions; at other times, Hogg ends abruptly, leaving the supernatural effect uppermost in the reader's mind. In fact, the constant tension between belief and unbelief is Hogg's most successful accomplishment. Probably the greater number of Hogg's supernatural stories should be taken literally, but a large enough number contain explained ghosts to keep the reader unsure. Knowing that Hogg may *not* explain away his effects, something disappointingly done in many Gothic novels, forces a more active and imaginative response by the reader, who can never be sure what Hogg will do.

Occasionally, the reader's reaction becomes integral to the story as in "The Barber of Duncow," which also illustrates Hogg's various uses of ghosts. The frame presents old Raighel, a tinkler's wife, deliberately setting out to attack her son-in-law, who thinks it absurd that "any reasonable being" should fear apparitions. She explains about her story that "when any body hears it, an disna believe it, the murdered woman is sure to come in." Then she tells of a barber, a lover of drink and women aptly named Roger M'Fun, who unaccountably marries a strict Cameronian girl, Grizel, given to prayers and psalms. A spirit appears to her one night and speaks of her great "family," Roger's illegitimate children. Grizel goes to see them, confronts her husband, and, after a great quarrel, disappears on the way home, never to be seen again. An inquiry concludes that the wife deserted her husband in disgust, and also discovers that the apparition was in fact a gypsy "who it was thought had good reason to ken about a part o' the bairns." This ghost, then, has a rational explanation.

Soon thereafter, however, Grizel with throat nearly severed appears to her old aunt, Janet Black, "ane liker a witch I [Raighel] never saw an auld crazed enthusiast she was." The ghost reveals how she had been slain by two women, one May Fiddes and one unknown to her, and her body sunk in a pool. Janet calls three village elders, who think her crazed with grief. But then, in the face of disbelief, Grizel's ghost appears to the men "in a far more frightful guise than it was the evening before. Its hands and its face were turned upwards, and the gash in its throat so much exposed, that it seemed as if the head were cut off all to the thickness of a man's thumb. At length it said, in an audible voice, that seemed to issue from the breast or the wound, and which sounded like the creaking of an hinge, 'He that believeth not Moses and the prophets, neither will he believe if one return from the dead. But, think you, a sister in faith would return from a world of spirits with a lie?'" The pool is dragged, and the body is recovered and brought to town where the townspeople are made to touch it. May refuses and collapses, though when her hand is pressed to the corpse, nothing happens; the barber then "began to treat the whole business with levity and contempt." But when the minister presses Roger's hand lightly to the body, immediately "the white sheet was bathed in a flood of purple blood that streamed from the wound, as if it had been newly inflicted." May eventually confesses that she and Roger had dressed as witches to frighten Grizel, but that the barber had gone on and killed her. Usually, Hogg's tale would end with the punishments of the guilty, but here he adds a final paragraph to round out the frame tale and add another turn of the screw. "This is the hale story of the barber," says Raighel; "but the most curious part is, that if the tale be accurately tould, and one of the hearers or more should doubt of its verity, the ghost o' poor Grizel to this day comes in in the same guise, and gives its testimony." Suddenly, the baby and dogs take fright, Raighel starts and says, "Hush! what's that at the door?" and the story ends.[6]

This tale illustrates almost all Hogg's typical uses of ghosts. The first, rationally explicable, comes to reveal an immoral act; the second exposes its own murder by telling where the corpse can be found and the identity of the killers, according to its own limited knowledge; and the folk tradition of the corpse which bleeds when touched by its murderers serves as final confirmation of the guilty party. In "The Unearthly Witness," a ghost summoned in court magically appears in the witness box to accuse a murderer. In "Julia M'Kenzie," the heroine's ghost confronts the clan leaders

who had thrown her off a bridge, though here she turns out to
have been saved by a miller and to have only disguised herself as a
ghost.[7] And in a score of other stories the ghosts defend justice,
returning to give warnings or to expose murder, cheating, and
immorality. Very rarely do they appear only for horrific effect. In
"Barber of Duncow" Hogg uses the frame story as a comic and
immediate warning against disbelief. Since the country people,
themselves firm believers, usually act as narrators or participants
in the opening dialogue, the tone of these tales is consistently one
of honest, objective, and complete acceptance of facts, simply and
truthfully narrated.

Ghosts are the most common supernatural figures in Hogg's
works; fairies and such like appear but rarely in pieces having a
realistic basis. However, they too expose evil and protect the
innocent. The ballad "Lyttil Pynkie" tells of such a sprite, a
beautiful little girl who appears one day in Kilbogye and, refusing
the Baron's advances, begins to sing a song "not framit of yirthly
wordis,/Though it soundit sweitte and shrill," a song about an
"elfynis fairye ryng." Then she begins a dance in which the Baron
collapses and dies; the chaplain and his men, having come to pick
up the body, also become caught up and danced to death as well.
Lyttil Pynkie takes the keys to the castle until the great Mass John
comes to exorcise her; but Pynkie explains:

> That fader wals ane man so wylde,
>   Disgraice of human fraime;
> Hee keipit sevin lemanis in his halle,
>   And maide it house of shaime;
> And his fat chapplyng—worste of alle,
>   Theyre dedis I maye not naime.

Knowing of John's goodness, she consigns him the Baron's
daughters,

> For oh there is moche for me to doo
>   'Mong maydenis mylde and meike;
> Men are so wycked heire belowe,
>   And wemyng are so weake.

Before leaving she bathes the priest's eyes to enable him to see the
evil at work throughout the invisible world, and indeed "half the

scenis the kirke withyeen/Were synnfulle and uncouthe" (*Poems*, 367-71). Here again the mischievous elf appears in defense of innocence, not only to expose the specific licentiousness of the Baron and his chaplain, but the evils throughout the world.

Witches occur more frequently than fairies in the tales, and they range from good to evil, and from truly supernatural to just old, strange women. Again, though, most of Hogg's witches are agents of good, and the others tend to be comic rather than evil. Ellen and Clara in "The Hunt of Eildon," having been kidnapped by witches, turn themselves into magic white hounds to effect acts of good; they can also transform other people: the misanthropic glutton, Croudy, is turned into a boar and nearly eaten, and the hero and heroine are changed into moorfowl to escape their persecutors. Ellen and Clara find themselves involved—like Robert Wringhim but apparently *with* divine sanction—in a "woful work of annihilation" so that the evil principle shall not "prevail in this little world of man, in which [they] have received for a time a willing charge" (*Tales*, 231). At the end, having preserved the lovely Pery from a charge of witchcraft, they return to their home, but find their mother newly married to a rude fortune hunter, and themselves treated with jealousy and hate, so they walk to a fairy ring and take leave of the sinful and impure world forever. Another of Hogg's enchanting heroines appears in "A Story of the Black Art," an incoherent love story in which Lady Elizabeth uses her ability to change form first to convince her father to take her from the convent in which she has been raised, then to tease her friend's husband, and finally to get herself a noble spouse. Inconsequential in theme, this entertaining tale does show a real practitioner of the black art who uses her powers for no evil purposes and who proves indeed to be "a most exemplary wife, and mother of a fine family."[8]

Brownies and bogles (goblins, probably the origin of "bogeymen"), being more like human beings, lend themselves to rational explanation more readily than other fairy creatures. Hogg's famous Brownie of Bodsbeck turns out to be but John Brown, a Cameronian wounded and deformed at the battle of Bothwell Bridge and now in hiding from Clavers. Katharine's trafficking with the devils is simply her giving supplies to the hunted men, despite their beliefs being different from her father's. But Walter commends her, saying, "Deil care what side they war on, Kate! ye hae taen the side o' human nature; the suffering and the humble side, an' the side o' feeling, my woman, that bodes best in a young unexperienced thing to tak. It is better than to do like yon bits o' gillflirts about Edinburgh; poor shilly-shally milk-an'-water things!" (*Tales*, 59). If the disguise of the Brownie seems merely a means of self-preservation, it nevertheless serves as a force for good, not only in the salvation of the poor hunted Cameronians, but in the rescue of Katharine from the hypocritical Clerk. Moreover, the disguise would have been less effective had there not been a strong belief in the Brownie's existence which Hogg stresses throughout. The *Brownie* is one of the few ghostly tales where the revelation of the ghost's existence does not disappoint, because the Brownie could well exist; it is as if Brown merely disguised himself as a real person anyway. Another nice disguise occurs in the comic love story "The Bogle o' the Brae; a Queer Courting Story," in which the two lively heroines, Barbary and Jane Bell, appear as ghosts and headless figures in order to drive away undesirable suitors and to take revenge on their proud and malicious rivals.[9]

Whether the spirits exist or not, Hogg always focuses on the human characters, both guilty and innocent, as they respond to these messages from the invisible world. Such treatments mark the beginnings, tentative to be sure with Hogg, of the use of terror to explore the human psyche. Dreams, for example, so pervade Hogg's works that they need not be discussed in detail except to observe that he uses them for plot rather than psychological insight, since the dreams (which may be symbolic) all indicate the future and all prove true. Hence, Queen Hynde dreams of being pursued by a black bull, and the pagan invader uses a black bull for his symbol; Cherry dreams of being abandoned by M'Ion on the precipice of the Rock of Love, and she dies after renouncing him in *Three Perils of Woman*; and George Dobson is only one of a number of characters warned of imminent destruction because of their sinful lives. These dreams are glimpses of an ordained future, as Queen Hynde realizes: "She saw a foresight had been given/To her of future things by Heaven" (*Poems*, 201). Perhaps the most interesting use of this device occurs in "Cousin Mattie," where seven-year-old Mattie dreams of an old woman warning that her cousin Sandy "will kill you; and on this day fortnight, you will be lying in your coffin, and that pale rose upon your breast." Sandy is sent away, nothing happens, and the boy becomes Mattie's great friend. Some years later Mattie dreams that Sandy's now-dead mother warns her "by all means to avoid her son, otherwise he was destined to be my murderer; and on that day seven-night I should be lying in my coffin."[10] This time Mattie goes away to avoid danger. Much later, however, Mattie does die on the day precisely fourteen years after the first dream, seven after the second. Sandy does not attend the funeral, and rumor has it that a pale baby had been buried with Mattie in the coffin. If Hogg's dreams do not reveal character, they nevertheless show the inexorable workings of fate or predestination which can neither be denied nor disregarded.

Other tales show the much more damaging effects of confrontations with the supernatural by characters with minds already somewhat deranged. "The Brownie of the Black Haggs," for instance, studies the obsession of a proud, tyrannical woman who delights in persecuting those of a religious nature. Finally, Lady Wheelhope takes to murdering those who displease her, a serving-maid and a poor village boy, although no charges can be proved. But new servants include the strange little Merodach, with "the form of a boy, but the features of one a hundred years old, save that his eyes had a brilliancy and restlessness which were very extraordinary" (*Tales*, 320). Immediately, Lady Wheelhope hates him, but she can never strike him: a poker she throws in a rage misses and breaks all the crockery on a shelf; an attempt to poison him fails when he feeds the milk to her favorite spaniel; finally, she tries to stab him in his bed, but mixes up the rooms and kills her son. But she protests against Merodach's dismissal, raving of revenge. Finally, she begins to follow him about, though he beats her unmercifully and tries to drive her away; she continually escapes, however, and is last seen "following the uncouth creature up the water of Daur, weary, wounded, and lame, while he was all the way beating her" (335). Later, a band of Covenanters finds her broken and mangled body, though the Brownie, as he came to be known, is never more seen. Though seemingly a demon—he throws aside an old servant's Bible—he nevertheless defeats another fiend, a victim, as Hogg says, of the "passion of inveterate malice" (335). But the most intriguing description occurs when the lady fixes her eyes on Merodach: "It was not a look of love nor of hatred exclusively, neither was it of desire or disgust, but it was a combination of them all" (334). An evil obsession faced by a reflection of its own evil leads not only to destruction, but to a masochistic end, as the Brownie serves as both object of revenge and symbol of her own guilt.

Hogg only touches on the psychological aberrations of Lady Wheelhope, recognizing the symptoms instinctively, perhaps, without being capable of further analysis, but the story suggests what might be done with the psychology of the supernatural. Also intuitively, but equally powerfully, Hogg begins to work with psychological doubles, again usually as a story device rather than as a theme. The briefest such tale is the "Strange Letter of a Lunatic," purportedly sent to Hogg by James Beatman to explain his confinement in an asylum. Beatman tells of meeting an old man one morning in Edinburgh and taking a pinch of snuff, much to the stranger's glee. Shortly thereafter Beatman comes face to face with a being identical to himself, but the other runs away. Later he comes across the double at a tavern, finds the double watching him, and hears him identify himself as James Beatman. The story progresses through a series of encounters, often with the double preceding the narrator to a place of rest or business. The narrator becomes completely confounded: "here was another being endowed with the same personal qualifications, who looked as I looked, thought as I thought, and expressed what I would have said. . . . I had become, as it were, two bodies, with only one soul between them, and felt that some decisive measures behoved to be resorted to immediately, for I would much rather be out of the world than remain in it on such terms." He challenges the double to a duel, but when they reach the field, the double accuses him of trying to take over *his* life. Finally, at the duel, "We fired at six paces distance, and I fell. Rather a sure sign that I *was* the right James Beatman, but which of the I's it was that fell I never knew till this day, nor ever can." Curious, Hogg seeks more information from a friend who reports that Beatman was seen entering the dell alone, that there were two shots, "yet there was no other man there that any person knew of, and still it was quite impossible that the pistol could have been fired by his own hand."[11] Hogg offers no explanations about the affair, other than Beatman's speculations about the old man in a dream; the story seems almost a technical exercise—a curious idea developed only narratively, with neither enough explanation nor analysis of

Beatman's character to allow for significant interpretation. Yet the eerie details work effectively on that narrative level, and in Poe, Dostoevsky, Stevenson, and Conrad the double would become an important recurring motif throughout the century.

## IV   *The* Confessions

Supernatural occurrences, doubles, autobiography, history, and comedy, along with a new interest in psychological analysis and a heightened narrative sophistication, all combine to produce Hogg's acknowledged masterpiece, *The Private Memoirs and Confessions of a Justified Sinner*. Virtually ignored when it first appeared—the only contemporary review assigned it to the class of "Scottish novels of the third rate," while contending that it neither instructs nor amuses (*Con*, 256-57)—it was mercilessly edited for the 1837 *Tales*, and it remained in this mutilated form for nearly a century. A centenary edition in 1924, however, eventually came into the hands of André Gide, who asked in the introduction to a 1948 reprint, "How explain that a work so singular and so enlightening, so especially fitted to arouse passionate interest both in those who are attracted by religious and moral questions, and, for quite other reasons, in psychologists and artists, and above all in surrealists who are so particularly drawn by the demoniac in every shape—how explain that such a work should have failed to become famous?"[12] For the past decades, though, the *Confessions* rather than the poetry has maintained Hogg's reputation and has led, curiously, to the renewal of interest in his other work. Essentially, the novel is a religious parable which derives from Hogg's firm moral beliefs, as well as from his faith in folk wisdom and his acceptance of the inexplicable in everyday life; the novel gains impact, however, from the tightly constructed plot, the artful blend of narrative devices, and an unusual emphasis upon psychological analysis.

The straightforward story, a remarkable thing in itself considering Hogg's other extended narratives, concerns Robert Wringhim, brought up in the strict Calvinist principles of his mother, Lady Dalcastle, and her spiritual adviser, the Rev. Robert Wringhim, probably the boy's natural father. Becoming convinced that he is one of God's elect—"adopted among the number of God's children . . . and that no bypast transgression, nor any future act of my own, or of other men, could be instrumental in altering the decree" (115)—Robert meets a young man, Gil-Martin, who advocates the same principles and supports them with even more arguments. Encouraged by this friend, Robert embarks on a series of righteous murders, convinced that he is carrying out God's will in removing the wicked from the earth. After killing a respected preacher, and allowing another to take the blame, he harasses his elder brother, George Colwan, and finally murders him; shortly thereafter the old laird dies of grief, and Robert inherits Dalcastle. He now begins to suffer from periods of amnesia, waking to find himself accused of various legal and moral crimes. Finally, about to be charged with the murders of his mother and a girl he had seduced, he runs away, helped but also pursued by Gil-Martin, whom Robert has grown to loathe. Every refuge he manages to find becomes haunted by strange noises and terrible demons until Robert is expelled; finally he hangs himself. When his grave is opened nearly a century later—as reported by a letter from Hogg in *Blackwood's*—the corpse and clothing appear fresh; the grave also contains the manuscripts which make up the bulk of the novel: Robert's printed confessions, set into type during a brief respite from his flight, and the diary of his last days.

If the story seems simple enough, the method of its telling is far more complex. Robert's confessions follow a ninety-page "Editor's Narrative," which sets forth most of the events according to traditional and historical sources. This section details the comic conflict between the old laird and his wife, the antagonism between Robert and George in Edinburgh which leads to the latter's death, and, finally, the efforts of the old laird's mistress, Arabella Logan, and a prostitute, Bell Calvert, to bring Robert to justice. The Editor returns briefly at the end to tell of opening the grave and to speculate on the meaning of the book. The confessions proper, however, do not merely retell the events, for Robert enlarges on his boyhood and tells of murdering Rev. Blanchard, before relating his own version of events in Edinburgh. Robert also adds considerably to his life at Dalcastle, and, of course, provides all the details of his flight from the estate until his decision to take his own life. In fact, only about a quarter of Robert's narrative duplicates the Editor's, and it corroborates most of the facts, as, for example, when Robert notes that he prayed three times a day and seven times on the Sabbath (100), an intensification of the Editor's contention that the boy prayed twice daily (18).

The events in Edinburgh naturally appear from Robert's point of view, as he rationalizes and distorts his actions—in disrupting his brother's tennis game, in attempting to push him over the side of Arthur's Seat, and finally in stabbing him. The Editor gives the latter scene according to Mrs. Calvert, who sees Robert stab his brother twice in the back while George duels with Gil-Martin. Robert, however, tells how he leapt between the two combatants: "To it we went, with full thirst of vengeance on every side. The duel was fierce; but the might of heaven prevailed, and not my might. The ungodly and reprobate young man fell, covered with wounds, and with curses and blasphemy in his mouth, while I escaped uninjured." The next paragraph, though, undercuts this heroic account, for Robert admits, "I will not deny, that my own immediate impressions of this affair in some degree differed from this statement. But this is precisely as my illustrious friend [Gil-Martin] described it to me afterwards, and I can rely implicitly on his information, as he was at that time a looker-on, and my senses all in a state of agitation, and he could have no motive for saying what was not the positive truth" (171).

Among the several reasons for Hogg's complicated narration, the most obvious is the attempt to establish reality in the traditional manner of eighteenth-century fiction, through an old manuscript and a skeptical narrator. The device removes the actual author, protecting him from being associated not only with belief in the supernatural but also with sacrilege. Too, Hogg publishes the novel anonymously and includes himself as a character—two other means of removing authorial responsibility. His narrative method also sets up important contrasts in a book of contrasts. The Editor's sections, for instance, contain most of the humor, in the account of the old laird and his wife and in the encounter with "James Hogg" at the end; these humorous elements throw into harsher light the dour, humorless and monomaniac life of Robert, who reports the speeches of comic servants but never sees them as funny. Finally, by emphasizing the multiple perspectives of events—through observers like Mrs. Calvert, biased participants like Robert, and after-the-fact historians like the Editor—Hogg reinforces one of his main concerns: the difficulty of perceiving anything accurately. Bell Calvert, for instance, recounting the story of George's murder, contends that the accomplice was not a suspected young cavalier despite the resemblance: "We have nothing on earth but our senses to depend upon: if these deceive us, what are we to do. I own I cannot account for [the resemblance]; nor ever shall be able to account for it as long as I live" (80). Later, Mrs. Logan restates that belief, adding, "Whose word, or whose reasoning can convince us against our own senses?" (85). Yet Robert's narrative proves that Gil-Martin was his accomplice, and legal evidence later establishes the innocence of young Drummond. Likewise, Robert later records the opinions of the villagers about his actions "to show how the best and greatest actions are misconstrued among sinful and ignorant men" (194). It's an ironic comment, part of Robert's own self-deception about his acts, but it also suggests how misunderstanding—whether by "rational" observers such as the two women and the Editor or by the deluded Robert—becomes an important part of Hogg's fictional world. Finally, only the reader can perceive all the facts of the story: factual, psychological, supernatural.

The use of fictional narrators other than Hogg in his role of storyteller or some other projected self-image also allows the author to create a novel far more unified than his other fiction. Everything in the tale, whether direct narration or interpolated story, goes to develop Robert's character and to point Hogg's warnings of the dangers of extremism. Being committed to the deluded fanatic on the one hand and the inquisitive Editor on the other allows Hogg to focus on his simple series of incidents with a breadth and depth of insight that indeed seems modern. Moreover, by restraining Hogg's own storytelling tendencies and his own buoyant good humor—both narrators are noticeably humorless—the narrative focus allows Hogg to develop his parable primarily through characterization.

Hogg begins by presenting his characters in conventional pairs of good and evil, moral and immoral, natural and unnatural. The two brothers, George and Robert, form the clearest pair: one seems all that is vital, healthy, and natural, while the other appears sullen, weak, and alienated; one is the son and heir, the other the illegitimate child. George "was a generous and kind-hearted youth; always ready to oblige, and hardly ever dissatisfied with any body," but Robert "was early inured to all the sternness and severity of his pastor's arbitrary and unyielding creed. . . . He was an acute boy, an excellent learner, had ardent and ungovernable passions, and withal, a sternness of demeanour from which other boys shrunk. . . . George was much behind him in scholastic acquirements, but greatly his superior in personal prowess, form, feature, and all that constitutes gentility in deportment and appearance" (18-19). In this essential contrast lie the seeds of fratricide: each has the tendency toward extremes, George with his carousing and Robert with his praying, but only George can see the possibility of reconciliation. Their antipathy toward one another, however, emerges immediately and results not so much from their personal situation—although Robert has been trained to despise both his brother and his legal father—but from the differing world-views they represent. George is Tom Jones; Robert, Blifil.

The extremes toward which they tend derive from the other dominant pair in the first part of the book, the elder George Colwan, laird of Dalcastle, and his wife, Rabina, the "reputed" daughter of a Glasgow baillie. The laird, too, derives from Fielding, a Scottish Squire Western, "a 'droll, careless chap,' with a very limited proportion of the fear of God in his heart, and very nearly as little of the fear of man. . . . He had hitherto believed that he was living in most cordial terms with the greater part of the inhabitants of the earth, and with the powers above in particular . . ." (2). His lady, however, "had imbibed her ideas from the doctrines of one flaming predestinarian divine alone; and these were so rigid, that they became a stumbling-block to many of his brethren" (2). Their wedding, celebrated with dancing, piping, singing, and feasting, becomes one of Hogg's fine comic scenes as the appalled wife first disappears, then forces her impatient husband into a series of prayers before retiring to their conjugal bed. Protesting against the prayer, the laird meets solid resistance: "against the cant of the bigot or the hypocrite, no reasoning can aught avail. If you would argue until the end of life, the infallible creature must alone be right. So it proved with the laird. One Scripture text followed another, not in the least connected, and one sentence of the profound Mr. Wringhim's sermons after another, proving the duty of family worship, till the laird lost patience, and, tossing himself into bed, said, carelessly,

that he would leave that duty upon her shoulders for one night"
(5). Ingloriously, the laird falls asleep, his snores drowning out his
bride's readings. Thus, in comic miniature, Hogg presents the
conflict and, indeed, the temporary triumph of the infallible bigot
over the natural man.

The family pairs continue this conflict: the two George Colwans
who love their pleasures but know their manners; the two Robert
Wringhims who love their prayers and glory in their own justified
state; even the two couples who manage to establish their domains
on the upper and lower levels of the house—the laird pairs with
Miss Arabella Logan, who moves in as his "housekeeper" but can
usually be found sitting on his knee, while Lady Dalcastle
occupies the third story, closer to heaven and farther from the real
world, spending her time with the Rev. Mr. Wringhim discussing
the "eight different kinds of FAITH, all perfectly distinct in their
operations and effects. But the lady, in her secluded state, had
discovered other five,—making twelve [sic] in all: the adjusting of
the existence or fallacy of these five faiths served for a most
enlightened discussion of nearly seventeen hours; in the course of
which the two got warm in their arguments, always in proportion
as they receded from nature, utility, and common sense" (12).
Arabella Logan later combines with Arabella Calvert, a prostitute,
to attempt to avenge the deaths of the laird and his son by
bringing young Wringhim to justice. With this pair, Hogg shows
the inherent goodness, kindness, and sense of justice which can
exist in two types of supposedly "immoral" women: a loving and
loyal mistress and a common street woman whose story also elicits
sympathy for the seduced and abandoned girl forced to beggary
and prostitution to feed herself and her child. ("My crimes have
been great, but my sufferings have been greater. . . . Mine have
been crimes of utter desperation," she tells Mrs. Logan.) By comparison, the horrors perpetrated by the Wringhims and Lady
Dalcastle in the name of morality and Christianity become even
more intolerable.

Before turning to the main pair of the second part of the novel,
Gil-Martin and Robert, some consideration should be given to the
series of comic figures—some of the best in Hogg's works—who
supply running commentary on the events of the novel. Though
they have their importance in establishing the parable, they also
serve to comment on the other characters as well as to help lighten

the predominantly somber tone. The first of these characters, Lady Dalcastle's father, appears but briefly. After Rabina returns to Glasgow following the disastrous wedding night, her father determines the cause of the disruption and announces his decision to his astonished child: "An' sae I find that Dalcastle has actually refused to say prayers with you when you ordered him; an' has guidit you in a rude indelicate manner, outstepping the respect due to my daughter,—as my daughter. But wi' regard to what is due to his own wife, of that he's a better judge nor me. However, since he has behaved in that manner to *my daughter*, I shall be revenged on him for aince; for I shall return the obligation to ane nearer to him; that is, I shall take pennyworths of his wife" (9). And the baillie "began to inflict corporal punishment on the runaway wife. His strokes were not indeed very deadly, but he made a mighty flourish in the infliction, pretending to be in a great rage only at the Laird of Dalcastle" (9). This sequence reinforces, as if the reader would need much further evidence, the unnatural behavior of Lady Dalcastle's putting theological niceties above the necessities of human living.

The second of these purely comic characters, Mrs. Logan's maid Bessy Gillies, amuses the courtroom audience with her "flippant and fearless" manner as she refuses to give absolute evidence against the accused thief, Belle Calvert. Recalling her mistress's lamentations—"We are baith ruined and undone creatures"—Bessy tells how she reacted: "The deil a bit; . . . that I deny postively. H'mn! to speak o' a lass o' my age being ruined and undone! I never had muckle except what was within a good jerkin, an' let the thief ruin me there who can" (66). Bessy refuses to believe that a woman's fingers could have broken the locks, and she will not identify the silver as her mistress's: though the spoons are all marked with a "C," she observes, "Sai are a' the spoons in Argyle, an' the half o' them in Edinburgh I think. A C is a very common letter, an' so are a' the names that begin wi't" (67). She also points out the inescapable fact that the prisoner's, not the plaintiff's, initials appear on the spoons. Again, folk wisdom—natural charity and justice—triumphs over the purely legalistic.

The last of these comic foils is Robert's servant, the Cameronian Samuel Scrape, who provides some shrewd rationalizing over taking pay twice for the same length of service: "In sic a case as this, sir, it disna hinge upon principles, but a piece o' good manners; an' I can tell you that at sic a crisis, a Cameronian is a gayan weel-bred man. He's driven to this, that he maun either make a breach in his friend's good name or in his purse; an' O, sir, whilk o' thae, think you, is the most precious? . . . The Cameronian then turns out to be a civil man, an' canna bide to make the man baith a feele an' liar at the same time, afore a' his associates; an' therefore he pits his principles aff at the side, to be a kind o' sleepin partner, as it war, an' brings up his good breeding to stand at the counter" (195). Samuel and Bessy stand as humorous warnings against the unbending principles of the Wringhims which breach not only good manners but common sense and joy in life. Samuel continues to play a kind of wise fool to Wringhim, when he recalls having been hired by Robert himself, "unless ye hae twa persons o' the same appearance, and twa tongues to the same voice" (195).

Another minor comic figure of note is "James Hogg," the author of a letter to *Blackwood's*, dated from Altrive Lake on August 1, 1823. "It bears the stamp of authenticity in every line," writes the Editor, "yet, so often had I been hoaxed by the ingenious fancies displayed in that Magazine, that when this relation met my eye, I did not believe it" (245). This actual letter, which appeared the year before the novel, spurs the search which eventually leads the Editor to a meeting with the Ettrick author at the ewe market at Thirlestone, after having been assured that "Hogg has imposed as ingenious lies on the public ere now" (246). The Shepherd, however, proves less than tractable, not believing the Editor's pose as a wool merchant and professing to be more interested in selling his stock than in showing the site of the grave: "I hae mair ado than I can manage the day, foreby ganging to houk up hunder-year-auld banes" (247). "Finding that we could make nothing of him," the Editor says, "we left him with his *paulies*, Highland stotts, grey jacket, and broad blue bonnet, to go in search of some other guide" (247). From the new guide, possibly the William Beattie of "A Shepherd's Wedding" (261n.), the Editor learns that Hogg's directions are completely misleading: the guide "added that it was a wonder how the poet could be mistaken there, who once herded the very ground where the grave is, and saw both hills from his own windows" (248). In this unhelpful figure, then, Hogg presents the extreme of the detached author, one who deliberately misleads, who refuses to help in the unraveling of the mystery which he himself first presented to the public.

Neither can the Editor, as the above anecdote indicates, be taken as a reliable guide to the events of the novel. Though he relates the first part of the story according to tradition and test-imony (without giving any specific sources) in a fairly straight-forward way, it becomes clear that he is only a dilettante re-searcher, interested more out of morbid curiosity than out of any great desire for seeking out truth. Indeed, his response to Hogg's letter suggests less than honorable motives about visiting the area: "from the moment that I perused it, I half formed the resolution of investigating these wonderful remains personally, if any such existed; for, in the immediate vicinity of the scene, as I supposed, I knew of more attractive metal than the dilapidated remains of mouldering suicides" (245). Revealing himself as a college friend of John Gibson Lockhart, he thus places himself in the educated upper classes, as opposed to the shepherd "Hogg." The Editor represents the modern, rational man—a gentleman, an intelligent if perhaps shallow individual limited by his empirical outlook. Though not perhaps a completely satirical figure as some critics suggest—his opening narrative is relatively unbiased, since most of the opinions which seem favourable to the Colwans are sub-stantiated by other witnesses—the Editor nevertheless comes to express disbelief. He cannot accept the supernatural events, con-cluding that "in this day, and with the present generation, it will not go down, that a man should be daily tempted by the devil, in the semblance of a fellow-creature" (254). Gil-Martin occurs in the Editor's narrative only as a mysterious but minor figure with little hint of the unusual about him. At the end, the Editor believes the book to be a failure, "a bold theme for an allegory, which would have suited the age well had it been taken up by one fully qualified for the task, which this writer was not" (254). In the absence, then, of reliable guides to the parable—"Hogg" selling his sheep and the Editor pursuing his more attractive metal—the reader remains the only one able to piece together the whole significance of Robert Wringhim's confessions.

Unlike the Editor, the reader must first come to terms with the character of Gil-Martin, another of Hogg's fine achievements; as Walter Allen notes, "it is doubtful whether a more convincing representation of the power of evil exists in our literature."[13]

Sophisticated, ironic, persuasive, with piercing eyes and the ability
to change his features at will, Gil-Martin first appears the very
day Robert believes himself among the saved—thus Hogg clearly
establishes the affinity between that belief and the Prince of Darkness. Gil-Martin has a regal bearing—his distinctive turban
resembles a bishop's miter—and Robert thinks him a prince of
some great kingdom, calling him "great potentate" and "great
sovereign." Robert also learns that Gil-Martin has no parents
"save one, whom I do not acknowledge" (129). His theology
emphasizes predestination—every action has been foreordained
and therefore God assumes responsibility—and other doctrines
such as the infallibility of the elect, salvation by grace, and the
divine mission of extermination to be undertaken. His proposal
for the first murder shows his Satanic sophistry: "If the man
Blanchard is worthy, it is better that one fall, than that a thousand
should perish [through the minister's "evil" influence]. For me,
my resolution is taken; I have but one great aim in this world, and
I never for a moment lose sight of it" (134). Irony, as the last
sentence indicates, pervades Gil-Martin's every remark: "Are all
your subjects Christians, prince?" asks Robert; "All my European subjects are, or deem themselves so," replies Gil-Martin;
"and they are the most faithful and true subjects I have" (136).
Though recognizing his friend's "subtility" of argument (134),
Robert never sees the irony, for doing so would mean admitting
the fearful nature of his companion.

With his ability to change his appearance, however, Gil-Martin
takes on even more significance: besides imitating others in order
that they be wrongfully accused—as with the preacher convicted
of Blanchard's murder and the gallant accused of killing George
—Gil-Martin most often takes the form of Robert or, toward the
end of the novel, of his dead brother. When they first meet,
Robert reacts with amazement: "he was the same being as myself;
The clothes were the same to the smallest item. The form was the
same; the apparent age; the colour of the hair; the eyes; and, as
far as recollection could serve me from viewing my own features
in a glass, the features too were the very same. I conceived at first,
that I saw a vision, and that my guardian angel had appeared to
me at this important era of my life." Gil-Martin's first words con-
firm the duality: "You think I am your brother, or that I am your
second self. I am indeed your brother, not according to the flesh,

but in my belief of the same truths" (117). From that point on Gil-Martin becomes as a shadow, though he never acts—in the murders, Gil-Martin's pistol misfires, so Robert must kill Blanchard, and Robert stabs his brother. Though the Father of Lies, Gil-Martin nevertheless explains to Robert a situation borne out in the novel: "We are all subjected to two distinct natures in the same person" (192). Earlier he had said, "Our beings are amalgamated, as it were, and consociated in one" (189). Gil-Martin thus represents the evil side of Robert's character, a Jungian shadow—inhuman, unforgiving, vengeful, and un-Christian. When he appears as the dead brother, he becomes, like Merodach, an external manifestation of Robert's guilt."[14]

Effective as this psychological doubling is, there can be little doubt that Hogg does not wish to explain away Gil-Martin's physical reality. Though he certainly seems a part of Robert and serves later as a visible reminder of his fratricidal guilt, Gil-Martin nevertheless functions as a being in his own right. His existence might seem to be at times explained by the overheated imaginations of the two avenging Arabellas or by Robert's apparent amnesia (he believes, for instance, that he has merely slept for one night, and he has no memory of the criminal and domestic acts carried out by himself or by one like him); but there remains too much evidence against Gil-Martin's being a mere delusion of Robert's distorted imagination. The first clue comes from the Editor's disbelief: such a pseudointellectual with no belief in the unseen can hardly be trusted, and his insistence that "no modern man could believe in temptation by the Devil" typifies those for whom metaphysical events no longer have real significance. Moreover, the two ladies see Gil-Martin with Robert on more than one occasion—indeed, the Devil winks at them and acknowledges their presence; other farmers and laborers, with whom Robert seeks refuge toward the end of his life, also experience all the supernatural horrors and enchantments perpetrated by the Devil's forces. Even the traditional accounts of the suicide indicate the presence of more than one person: "every one said, if the devil had not assisted him it was impossible the thing could have been done; for, in general, these ropes are so brittle, being made of green hay, that they will scarcely bear to be bound over the rick. And the more to horrify the good people of this neighborhood, the driver said, when he first came in view, *he could almost give his oath* that he saw two people busily engaged at the hay-rick, going round it and round it, and he thought they were dressing it" (242). As the above passage indicates, the most important identification both of Gil-Martin as the Devil and as a very real entity comes from the constant comments of the peasants: Samuel Scrape tells Robert how "the strange mysterious person that attended you, him that the maist part of folks countit uncanny, had gane awa wi' a Mr. Ringan o' Glasko last year, and had never returned" (186). Later, Samuel repeats the gossips' tales: "they say the deil's often seen gaun sidie for sidie w'ye, whiles in ae shape, an whiles in another. An' they say that he whiles takes your ain shape, or else enters into you, and then your turn a deil yoursel" (195). Such observations about Gil-Martin cannot be underrated.

Gil-Martin's reality, however, stands second to the portrait of Robert himself, Hogg's great achievement in the novel. Not merely the Editor's "greatest wretch," "greatest fool," or "religious maniac," Robert emerges as a believable human being warped by his background as well as by his beliefs. Had the novel consisted solely of the Editor's narrative, the story would remain a horrifying account of religion perverted to justify murder, fratricide, seduction, and matricide. The firsthand account, which shows how the doctrines become perverted, creates in addition a sympathetic picture of the young man who, without recognizing the error of his beliefs, nevertheless exhibits very human traits. Moreover, his early candor is refreshing as he relates his youthful adventures in confessional/didactic style. "I was born an outcast," Robert writes immediately (97), and an outcast he remains, rejected by his legal father and doomed by the severity of the elder Wringhim's principles never to partake of the social life of his contemporaries, of the companionship of women, indeed, of intercourse with all those deemed wicked. Even before meeting Gil-Martin, Robert receives a warning against overseverity from his father's servant, John Barnet, who calls him "a selfish and conceited blackguard, who made great pretences towards religious devotion to cloak a disposition tainted with deceit" (101). By lying, Robert succeeds in having Barnet dismissed from service, just as he succeeds in having a superior schoolmate, M'Gill, expelled from school; he justifies these petty revenges on religious grounds. Yet, he freely admits breaking commandments and being a sinner. His human reaction to Wringhim's early fear that the boy may not be one of the elect can be paralleled in many Calvinist writings: "My heart quaked with terror, when I thought of being still living in a state of reprobation, subjected to the awful issues of death, judgment, and eternal misery, by the slightest accident or casualty" (99-100). Likewise, his feeling of elation on becoming convinced of his salvation (116) resembles that of Jonathan Edwards on coming to understand God's power or, more ominously, that of Milton's Adam and Eve upon eating the forbidden fruit.

Indeed, the human frailties given Robert make him one of the most convincing characters in all Hogg's works. His envy of his schoolmate M'Gill—whose name, Douglas Gifford points out, reflects that of Robert's tempter,[15] a fact which again suggests Gil-Martin's reflection of Robert's guilt—leads Robert to imitate his drawing style and create lewd pictures of the schoolmaster to bring wrath upon his enemy's head. Later, Robert lies about M'Gill and causes him to be flogged and dismissed, whereupon M'Gill haunts Robert, as Gil-Martin will later, and as Robert haunts George. "That I was a great, a transcendent sinner, I confess. But still I had hopes of forgiveness, because I never sinned from principle, but accident; and then I always *tried* to repent of these sins by the slump, for individually it was impossible" (113). From these schoolboy perversions, Robert goes on to display other traits that heighten not only his unnaturalness but the warped nature of his upbringing. "In particular," he notes, "I brought myself to despise, if not to abhor, the beauty of women, looking on it as the greatest snare to which mankind are subjected, and though young men and maidens, and even old women, (my mother among the rest,) taxed me with being an unnatural wretch, I gloried in my acquisition; and to this day, am thankful for having escaped the most dangerous of all snares" (113). Later, when Robert has been accused of seducing a young woman, he protests, but confesses that, "highly as I disapproved of the love of women, and all intimacies and connections with the sex, I felt a sort of indefinite pleasure, an ungracious delight in having a beautiful woman solely at my disposal" (181). The excessive distrust of women which forms part of his religious tenets finds its outlet in the obscene pictures, the possible attack on the girl (whether perpetrated by Robert unconsciously or by Gil-Martin in

Robert's form), and the confession of the desire for power. Finally, Robert's masochistic tendencies can be seen in the way in which he invites insult and violence in forcing himself on his brother's society; the Editor reports, "They loaded him with execrations, but it availed nothing; he seemed courting persecution and buffetings. . . . He was such a rueful-looking object, covered with blood, that none of them had the heart to kick him, although it appeared the only thing he wanted" (24). Here the impulse toward martyrdom and humility has been perverted into a kind of aggressive innocence which affronts common humanity.

Moreover, as his deeds become more serious, so too do his doubts increase. Robert objects to the murder of Blanchard, but gives in to Gil-Martin's persuasion; in theory the carrying out of the Lord's mission seems fine, but in practice Robert has instinctive reservations: as they wait in ambush, Blanchard "came deliberately on, pausing at times so long, that we dreaded he was going to turn. Gil-Martin dreaded it, and I said I did, but wished in my heart that he might" (139). These heart-promptings reflect Hogg's belief in the innate goodness of even such a wretch as Robert. Later, in entertaining "doubts regarding the justification of all the deeds of perfect men" (168), Robert proposes to his friend "that I did not think the Scripture promises to the elect, taken in their utmost latitude, warranted the assurance that they could do no wrong; and that, therefore, it behoved every man to look well to his steps" (169). When Gil-Martin changes from a companionable adviser to a supercilious, exulting persecutor, Robert writes, "I began to have secret terrors, that the great enemy of man's salvation was exercising powers over me, that might eventually lead to my ruin" (182). The great horror of the *Confessions* is not merely that Robert misinterprets doctrine, but that he acts always in the belief of right. Indeed, he never ceases to believe in his capacity for benevolence. After inheriting Dalcastle, he says, "I immediately set about doing all the good I was able, hoping to meet with all approbation and encouragement from my friend. I was mistaken: He checked the very first impulses towards such a procedure, questioned my motives, and uniformly made them out to be wrong" (173). Even when fleeing from arrest, he says, "I had nevertheless hopes that, by preaching up redemption by grace, pre-ordination, and eternal purpose, I should yet be enabled to benefit mankind in some country, and rise to high distinction" (210). And at the end, in a fine recognition scene, Robert confesses, "I wept, thinking of what I might have been, and what I really had become: of my high and flourishing hopes, when I set out as the avenger of God on the sinful children of men; of all that I had dared for the exaltation and progress of the truth; and it was with great difficulty that my faith remained unshaken" (227). This faith, which keeps him from seeing the ultimate horror of his acts, must now be accounted merciful. If Robert is a hypocrite, a fanatic, a monster, a maniac, as those in and out of the book suggest, he is no such easy target as the lustful curate of *The Brownie of Bodsbeck* or the greedy monk of *Pilgrims of the Sun*; rather, he recalls the young preacher of "The First Sermon," humanly vulnerable and thereby the more pitiable.

All these touches which make Robert a very human victim of excessive ideologies, perverted beliefs, and warped upbringing bring the novel into the realm of human tragedy and save it from being merely a cautionary tale. Robert dies a suicide, a fate he considers but rejects earlier in the novel; even the Editor points out that he has "committed that act for which, according to the tenets he embraced, there was no remission, and which consigned his memory and his name to everlasting detestation" (255). This act confirms the Devil's final power over Robert, but it also stamps him as a human being pushed beyond his spiritual and psychological limits. His farewell stands as his most human and most moving utterance in the book and heightens the tragic ending: "Farewell, world, with all thy miseries; for comforts or enjoyments hast thou none! Farewell, woman, whom I have despised and shunned; and man, whom I have hated; whom, nevertheless, I desire to leave in charity! And thou, sun, bright emblem of a far brighter effulgence, I bid farewell to thee also!" (239). The human traits behind his inhumanity make him a truly tragic figure.

Yet the parable remains the most important part of the novel. Gide identifies the religious issue as the antinomian heresy, described in the *Dictionary of all Religions*: antinomians "say that good works do not further, nor evil works hinder salvation: that the child of God cannot sin, that God never chastiseth him, that murder, drunkenness, etc., are sins in the wicked but not in him, that the child of grace, being once assured of salvation, afterwards never doubteth.''[16] It seems unlikely that Hogg has any technical theological point to argue: he derides, for instance, the disputations between Lady Dalcastle and Rev. Wringhim as "the splitting of hairs, and making distinctions in religion where none existed" (16). And at the end of the book, when Robert passes himself off as a poor student of theology bound for Oxford, the innkeeper's family "stared at one another with expressions of wonder, disappointment, and fear [because] the term *theology* was by them quite misunderstood, and . . . they had some crude conceptions that nothing was taught at Oxford but the *black arts*, which ridiculous idea prevailed over all the south of Scotland" (230). Rather, Hogg wishes only to show the practical effects of carrying the beliefs in predestination and justification by grace to extremes. Nowhere does Hogg employ arguments beyond those that the most ordinary reader could follow—Gil-Martin's subtle arguments are merely summarized or described as being "unanswerable." Even the elder Wringhim's legendary retort to the old laird is not given, due to "the shackles of modern decorum" (15). As in the histories, Hogg explores not principles but the human results of the applications of those principles. The book warns not against Calvinism nor even literally against antinomianism; rather, it exposes the vice of unreasonable enthusiasm and upholds his often-preached ideals of moderation, common sense, and perfectibility.

Hogg again directs this warning to literate, intellectual readers, for country people have little need of such warnings, being instinctively on their guard. Wringhim's confessions contain a considerable number of warnings concerning his actions, most of them from people of good common sense. John Barnet saves Robert from a beating, though the boy had already cost the man his job, and illustrates charity, as does George in later offering to make peace. Climbing Arthur's Seat to kill George, Robert meets a woman in white: "I was just about to ask direction from above, when I heard as it were a still small voice close by me, which uttered some words of derision and chiding. [The lady] regarded me with a severity of look and gesture that appalled me so much, I could not address her; but she waited not for that, but coming close to my side, said, without stopping, 'Preposterous wretch! how dare you lift your eyes to heaven with such purposes in your heart? Escape homeward, and save your soul, or farewell for ever!'" (157-58). The timing and the "still small voice" both suggest the origin of this angelic being.

Other warnings refer specifically to Gil-Martin, whom the country people, as Samuel Scrape recounts, recognize instinctively as the Devil. When Robert flees Dalcastle, he first stops at a weaver's house, but the man is wary; "I was feared," he explains, "ye might be that waratch that the deil has taen the possession o', an' eggit him on to kill baith his father an' his mother, his only brother, an' his sweetheart" (212). Next morning, trying to escape from a locked room, Robert gets caught in the weaver's looms and becomes suspended upside down, a visual image of his reversed beliefs and his entanglement in the web of evil. In the last houses he visits, he is considered the devil himself, especially when fiends seem to rend and tear the outer walls.

Through the motif of prayer, Hogg reinforces the divisions between the characters as well as warning against the perversion of religious devotion. The laird's objections to prayers before retiring to the conjugal bed have already been noted, as has the bride's father's supporting belief. Robert's rather mechanical habit of praying "three times every day, and seven times on the Sabbath" seems to help him but little: "the more frequently and fervently that I prayed, I sinned still the more" (100). Clearly, his difficulty lies in the kind of prayer he makes, one that doubtless derives from Rev. Wringhim's teaching, for Hogg reports the good pastor's prayers in full and stresses their inhumanity, their lack of charity and compassion. After Robert inherits Dalcastle, for example, he and his adopted father return due thanks, which "consisted wholly in telling the Almighty what he was; and informing him, with very particular precision, what *they* were who addressed him; for Wringhim's whole system of popular declamation consisted it seems in this,—to denounce all men and women to destruction, and then hold out hopes to his adherents that they were the chosen few, included in the promises, and who could never fall away. It would appear that this pharisaical doctrine is a very delicious one, and the most grateful of all others to the worst characters" (56). The final comment again sounds more like Hogg than the Editor, and it also echoes John Barnet's denunciation. Earlier Wringhim had been pictured in evening prayer as praying "for so many vials of wrath to be poured on the head of some particular sinner, that the hearers trembled, and stopped their ears." He then proceeds to lead a hymn which curses the sinner and stresses vengeance. The narrator, also seemingly in Hogg's voice, comments that "it is a pity [these verses] should ever have been admitted into a Christian psalmody, being so adverse to all its mild and benevolent principles" (32).

More significantly, Gil-Martin refuses to pray at all, a practise which Robert notes, but fails to act on: "we had never once prayed together; and more than that . . . he had constantly led my attentions away from that duty, causing me to neglect it wholly" (128). Ten days before Robert's death, Gil-Martin does indeed provide the wretched being with "an ejaculatory prayer, which I was to pronounce, if in great extremity. I objected to the words as equivocal, and susceptible of being rendered in a meaning perfectly dreadful" (238). Indeed, by the end of the novel, Robert's prayers have changed from the mechanical and denunciatory to the humble and questioning, as he progresses toward a more human understanding of his plight. His early prayers for intercession have been selfish rationalizations; toward the end he prays with the weaver's family, and the wife approves though her husband tried to show "that every thing for which I had interceded in my prayer, was irrelevant to man's present state" (214). As his adversity increases, he "prayed that the Lord would hide me in the bowels of the earth, or depths of the sea" (229), and his final prayer echoes Job's humble but questioning faith as opposed to Wringhim's arrogant pride: "Lord, thou knowest all that I have done for thy cause on earth! Why then art thou laying thy hands so sore upon me? Why has thou set me as a butt of thy malice? But thy will must be done! Thou wilt repay me in a better world. *Amen*" (239). The repeated sufferings and warnings have had at least some effect.

The main warning, indeed one of Hogg's finest tales, comes from the Cameronian valet in the form of a parable about the village of Auchtermuchty which "grew so rigidly righteous, that the meanest hind among them became a shining light in ither towns an' parishes. There was naught to be heard, neither night nor day, but preaching, praying, argumentation, an' catechising in a' the famous town. . . . The young men wooed their sweethearts out o' the Song o' Solomon, an' the girls returned answers in strings o' verses out o' the Psalms" (198). One day a strange preacher enters the church and delivers a terrifying hellfire and damnation sermon to the approving congregation. Another sermon having been announced, the people gather round and "were amazed, and many of them went into fits, writhing and foaming in the state of the most horrid agitation [without perceiving] the ruinous tendency of the tenets so sublimely inculcated" (202). Finally, however, old Robin Ruthven, whose suspicions had been aroused by overhearing some crows talking about the imminent downfall of the village, lifts the preacher's gown to reveal a pair of cloven feet. "An' frae that day to this," Samuel concludes, "it is a hard matter to gar an Auchtermuchty man listen to a sermon at a', an' a harder ane still to gar him applaud ane, for he thinks aye that he sees the cloven foot peeping out frae aneath ilka sentence" (203). Plain and unsophisticated Robin has one advantage over the elders and supposed wise men of the town—"he had been in the hands o' the fairies" when young (198).

The religious parable that the Editor seeks in the *Confessions*, then, clearly reflects Hogg's own views of the supernatural and of the need for religious toleration and moderation. Evil exists in the world, as a function of man's dual nature; but it also derives from carrying the cause of goodness to extremes and from justifying one's actions in the name of good. The novel manifestly does not satirize Calvinism, for Hogg—himself a staunch Calvinist—puts the clearest statements of his main theme in the mouths of two orthodox believers: Scrape, the Cameronian, and Mr. Blanchard, who tells Robert, after meeting his friend, Gil-Martin,

There is a sublimity in his ideas with which there is to me a mixture of terror; and when he talks of religion, he does it as one that rather dreads its truths than reverences them. He, indeed, pretends great strictness of orthodoxy regarding some of the points of doctrine embraced by the reformed church; but you do not seem to perceive, that both you and he are carrying these points to a dangerous extremity. Religion is a sublime and glorious thing, the bond of society on earth, and the connector of humanity with the Divine nature; but there is nothing so dangerous to man as the wresting of any of its principles, or forcing them beyond their due bounds: this is of all others the readiest way to destruction. Neither is there any thing so easily done. There is not an error into which a man can fall, which he may not press Scripture into his service as proof of the probity of, and though your boasted theologian shunned the full discussion of the subject before me, while you pressed it, I can easily see that both you and he are carrying your ideas of absolute predestination, and its concomitant appendages, to an extent that overthrows all religion and revelation together; or, at least, jumbles them into a chaos, out of which human capacity can never select what is good. (131-32)

## V  Conclusion

How then to evaluate Hogg's claim to be "King o' the Mountain and Faery school"? Clearly, the supernatural impinges upon almost every facet of his work, giving it a richness and a significance, not to mention an interest that it might not otherwise have. The particularization of the unseen—the distinct spheres of influence of ghosts, brownies, fairies, wraiths, and other beings—suggests an intimate acceptance of that world rarely found in serious literature—an acceptance which allows more effective presentations. But the Shepherd never ignores the present world, as he shows invisible forces at work, changing, warning, influencing, exposing human actions. Hogg never follows the Matthew Lewis school of "horror for horror's sake"—gruesome details occur but rarely, and they always intensify the villainy, as in the monk of *Pilgrims*, or convince the unbelievers, as in the appearances of various ghosts; the actual horrors of the *Confessions* receive little specific attention, for only the sounds of demons outside the house are heard, and the terrors occur in the victim's and the reader's imaginations. Moreover, in using terror to investigate abnormal behavior, as in "Brownie of the Black Haggs," and to explore the literary use of the double, most successfully in the *Confessions*, Hogg anticipates the works of later writers.

Two other points remain. Hogg constantly raises questions of appearance and reality. Are supernatural visions optical delusions or have they a reality of their own? The person who dismisses them does so at his peril, for the visions in Hogg's stories are almost always beneficial. Dreams, wraiths, omens, fairies, and such dare not be ignored, and the evidence of the senses—even if it conflicts with reason—must be admitted. Hogg describes Sir Simon Brodie, for all his absurdity and monomania, as one of "those sensible men who never distrusted the evidence of his senses" (263), and if his mind cannot distinguish between a seal and a mermaid, his acceptance of strange events allows him an undeniable bravery and success in his exploits. "Welldean Hall" begins with a comic play of wit between two rustics that ends on a question of the appearance of their late master's ghost. It is not an imposition on people's senses, Gilbert asserts, for "A man has nothing but his external senses to depend on in this world. If these may be supposed fallacious, what is to be considered as real that we either hear or see? I conceive, that if a man *believes* that he *does* see an object standing before his eyes, and knows all its features and lineaments, why, he *does* see it, let casuists say what they will. If he hear it pronounce words audibly, who dare challenge the senses that God has given him, and maintain that he heard no such words pronounced? I would account the man a presumptuous fool who would say so, or who would set any limits to the phenomena of nature, knowing in whose hand the universe is balanced, and how little of it he thoroughly understands" (*Tales*, 160).

An example of this belief can be added from Hogg's own experiences. One of the most powerful scenes in the *Confessions* occurs on Arthur's Seat where George, meditating on the beauties of the morning mist, suddenly sees, "delineated in the cloud, the shoulders, arms, and features of a human being of the most dreadful aspect. The face was the face of his brother, but dilated to twenty times the natural size. . . . Its eyes were fixed on him, in the same manner as those of some carnivorous animal fixed on its prey; and yet there was fear and trembling, in these unearthly features, as plainly depicted as murderous malice. The Giant apparition seemed sometimes to be cowering down as in terror, so that nothing but its brow and eyes were seen" (41). George wheels about, terrified, and crashes into the real Robert about to kill him. Robert's account, however, mentions nothing; the giant figure, menacing and malicious, appears only to the sane man and saves him from death. The experience has its counterpart in an incident from Hogg's shepherd days; in "Nature's Magic Lantern," he recounts seeing on a foggy hillside "a huge dark semblance of the human figure, which stood at a very small distance from me, and at first appeared to my affrighted imagination as the enemy of mankind." He returns the next morning and sees "a giant blackamoor, at least thirty feet high, and equally proportioned, and very near me. I was actually struck powerless with astonishment and terror" (*Tales*, 459). When he takes off his

bonnet, perplexed whether to flee or stay and take care of his
lambs, the figure takes off its hat as well, and the nineteen-year-
old shepherd realizes that it is a reflection of his own person.
Thus, the situation in the *Confessions* may have a rational
explanation—outside the novel—but the time, manner, and
features of the figure's appearance suggest supernatural intervention. It may even be Gil-Martin, who often thwarts Robert's
schemes.

This point reveals Hogg's most important use of the supernatural: the ghostly agents not only show the palpable presence of
good and evil at work in the world, but show them as bound up in
the workings of God's orderly universe. Even when treating
ancient or allegorical worlds, Hogg does not present an idealized
past, since the same avarice, lust, immorality, and irreligion exist
then as now; the Devil makes his appearance, literally and figuratively, then as now. By linking the world of faery with the
Christian world, Hogg shows an unbroken and complementary
relationship of all creatures pressing forward toward perfection.
Even the forces of evil cause good, though it be against their
nature. The monstrous apparition saves George Colwan, and Gil-
Martin repeatedly brings Robert to the notice of the authorities.
Other seemingly equivocal beings, such as ghosts, wraiths, fairies,
and brownies, constantly expose the guilty and protect the innocent.

Hogg also fears the extremes of reason, as of religion, when
used to disprove evidence of the senses. Hence the constant
criticism of the dialecticians—lawyers, theologians, intellectuals.
Wringhim's extremism does not necessarily result solely from
religion; it would be misplaced in whatever endeavor he attempted.
So Hogg's heroes and heroines resemble himself: country people
with clear common sense, simple but strong faiths in the nature of
God and the workings of his justice, and unquestioning acceptance of the evidence of the senses. Robin Ruthven, who lifts the
devil's gown at Auchtermuchty, represents all these people, Hogg's
people, in their natural intelligence. "The shepherd was more
enlightened than the worthy clergyman," Hogg writes in "The
Hunt of Eildon," "as shepherds generally are."[17] Hogg begins
"The Mysterious Bride" in 1830 with a clear assertion: "A great
number of people now-a-days are beginning broadly to insinuate
that there are no such things as ghosts, or spiritual beings visible

to mortal sight. Even Sir Walter Scott is turned renegade, and, with his stories made up of half and half, like Nathaniel Gow's toddy, is trying to throw cold water on the most certain, though most impalpable phenomena of human nature. The bodies are daft. Heaven mend their wits!" (*Tales*, 453).

# CHAPTER 7

# *Conclusion*

W ITHOUT doubt Hogg wrote too much; or, too many of the poorer works survive, embalmed in the double-columned standard edition. Paradoxically, though, many worthy works have been neglected—either buried in the edition or uncollected. Of his novels, *Confessions* is a masterpiece, but the two *Perils* also contain superb supernatural and romantic action, as well as impressive evocations of old Scotland; the long narrative poems have less to recommend them, perhaps, though many of the shorter pieces in *Queen's Wake* have interest and *Pilgrims* is central to an understanding of Hogg's notions of perfectibility and attitudes toward religion. Many of the comic and historical songs, a few of the reflective poems, several lyrics, and the major parodies of the *Poetic Mirror* would make up a volume that would do credit to any poet. Likewise, the best of the supernatural tales and many of the adventure stories—the novelettes often seem most successful ("Basil Lee," "John Lochy," "George Cochrane," "Sir Simon Brodie," "The Hunt of Eildon"), since Hogg has enough space to develop his characters and themes adequately without overcomplicating his plot—would provide a volume or two of quality fiction. Even his nonfiction writings, the best of which present a picture of pastoral life irrecoverably lost except in such literature, can stand on their own considerable merits.[1]

Despite the problems of his works' availability, Hogg has always been recognized by remarkable people. In his own time, of course, he was compared with Burns and Scott, for understandable if not completely valid literary reasons; and he was familiarly acquainted with many of his famous contemporaries—Scott, Wordsworth, and Southey, among others; he met Carlyle and corresponded with Byron. Moreover, his fame spread beyond

Britain: when Washington Irving visited Scott, "He was very anxious to see Hogg, and . . . always regretted that he had not met with the Shepherd."[2] The enormous popularity of *Blackwood's* also promoted his reputation, since it along with the Waverley novels formed the staple readings for the next generation of writers. Thus Charlotte Brontë begins her "History of the Year" by alluding to the *Blackwood's* writers, especially "James Hogg, a man of most extraordinary genius," and her more unstable brother wrote *Blackwood's* lamenting Hogg's death and offering himself as a replacement.[3] In America, Poe was intimately acquainted with *Blackwood's*, as his parodies, criticisms, and stories show; he doesn't mention Hogg, but alludes often to the *Noctes*.[4]

As Hogg's centenary passed, the *Confessions* became known to a few as his chief accomplishment, with both George Saintsbury and Edmund Gosse marveling that a man like Hogg could have written such a book, the former even suggesting that Hogg must have had Lockhart's help. In the early twentieth century, T. Earle Welby, in *A Study of Swinburne*, comments on the *Poetic Mirror*, that "wonderful and almost entirely unknown volume, which, with Swinburne's *Heptalogia*, shares the foremost place that can be accorded to genuine poetic parody."[5] Finally, of course, came André Gide's "discovery" of the *Confessions*, and his introduction speculating on whether Robert Browning knew the novel. Such notice suggests an appeal greater than that of a merely local talent.

## I  *Hogg and Scotland*

Sir James Douglas, in the "Famous Scots Series" at the turn of the century, calls Hogg "local rather than universal, the poet of a class rather than of humanity, of an epoch rather than of the ages." A quarter of a century later, Henry Thew Stephenson comments, "Until recently it seemed as if in the outside world the name of Hogg except to students of literature, would pass into oblivion along with that of Wilson; but the Forest still holds his fame secure."[6] Memorials of Hogg still exist in sparsely populated Ettrick—his grave in the parish church, an obelisk marking the site of his birth, a monument overlooking St. Mary's Loch, Tibbie Shiels's inn. But though a poet *from* Ettrick, Hogg was by no means a poet *of* Ettrick, as was, for example, Dorset's William Barnes or the Yukon's Robert Service. Hogg's observations of nature certainly derive from Ettrick experiences: poems such as the "Farewell to Ettrick" and "St. Mary of the Lowes" specify local landmarks, and the tales of the Covenanters use the hills and caves as hiding places. But, in fact, "Ettrick" as a setting does not go beyond such occasional descriptions; it is never a determining factor in theme or character—excepting the rural wisdom of its people.

Edinburgh plays a much larger role in the works, becoming perhaps the best-known location of his fiction—the setting for the greater part of two novels and for many tales, including the "Life of an Edinburgh Baillie." The third novel, set in the Lowlands during the Border Wars of the Middle Ages, and the long poems deal with vaguely medieval settings rather than realistically contemporary ones. In addition, the Highlands, which Hogg often happily visited, provide the background for *Mador*—originally written on a challenge from his Highland hostess—as well as for events of the Jacobite uprisings; even here, though, the Jacobites in hiding can hardly be distinguished from the Covenanters in hiding. Though he occasionally sends his characters to Africa, the North Pole, and North America, Hogg must be seen as a poet of his entire country; in *The Queen's Wake* he shows for contemporary readers, as well as for Queen Mary, the variety of regional songs and stories, and characters, all of which he was adept at imitating. Yet the sense of place—beyond its being Scotland—is rarely an important element in Hogg's works.

His essential Scottishness can be found in the tone of his writing, a facet of which G. Gregory Smith, in his seminal essays on Scottish literary history, designates as "the Caledonian antisyzygy"—a "combination of opposites" that forms the basis of the Scottish character and hence its literature. Noting the contrasts which the "Scot shows at every turn in his political and ecclesiastical history, in his polemical restlessness, in his adaptability," Smith suggests that "in his literature the Scot presents two aspects which appear contradictory."[7] Hogg's antisyzygy makes itself felt most strongly in the two constant tensions of his best work: fact and fiction, belief and unbelief. The mixtures of autobiography and fancy, of history and imagination, create a subjective reality that goes beyond either photographic realism or pure imagination; his use of himself, especially, or of images of himself, ties his stories to a convincingly real world. In dealing with the faery worlds, the combination of emotional belief and rational disbelief allows him to present some of the most compelling supernatural stories in English literature. They, too, are tied to a real world, but a world in which supernatural beings appear as another part of God's order. This reconciliation of two seemingly opposed realities gives Hogg's reader a sense of intimate acquaintance with and acceptance of a world beyond immediate ken.

## II  *Hogg's Achievement*

Yet Hogg's audience goes beyond Scotland. He published some works in London as well as in Edinburgh, and he reached America; even *Three Perils of Woman* was translated into French. His dialect pieces are usually intelligible to a non-Scot (except when he imposes the pseudomedieval Scots), since he wrote in the literary English of the time, and in the literary Scots—that printed dialect probably never spoken anywhere at any time but which approximates Scots, at least for English readers.[8] Such a wide audience is deserved, for he deals with subjects and with modes that have a timeless and universal appeal. Although intellectually unsophisticated, he could tell a story with such verve and believability that his themes become as effective as those of more complex writers.

Foremost among the achievements are the supernatural works. By telling ghostly tales through many different and sophisticated narrative techniques, Hogg achieves convincing representations of the invisible world. Hogg's ghosts do not terrify; they serve as part of a Divine plan that works toward the perfectibility of man—they warn the endangered, they expose the guilty, they unite with more traditional forces to bring about Divine justice. But, most important, they exist, exist as much as any fictional character. Gil-Martin, the good witches of Eildon, the Brownie of Bodsbeck convince the reader because they have convinced the author—with Hogg and his narrators never doubting, the reader too never doubts; and with their existence established, Hogg can go on to explore profound human characteristics—love, loyalty, guilt, pride, hypocrisy, vengeance—as well as man's mixture of humanity and inhumanity.

Hogg's main theme, too, has continuous application: the need for restraint, for moderation in the face of excess zeal. Whether that zeal be directed in the cause of religion or romance, education or poetry, Hogg stands ready, with the common sense of Mr. Blanchard or Robin Ruthven, to expose, to deflate, to tone down. Robert Wringhim's doctrinal excesses are more dangerous than but similar to Byron's romantic excesses and Wordsworth's reflective ones. The chivalric code of medieval times, like the social manners of Edinburgh, deforms humanity, restrains natural emotions, defeats the purpose of life: enjoying and responding naturally to it. In exposing such excesses, Hogg concentrates on women, showing them as victims but also as people, not romantic puppets, who can take a hand in their own destinies. Hogg's anti-romance is a function of his realistic outlook—he undercuts the idealism with glimpses of the human and actual.

Overseriousness about literature is also romantic—from Shelley through Joyce to the present day—so Hogg adopts instead the notion of literature as entertainment and instruction, the latter disguised by the former. His worst works, the pure exempla usually, involve mechanical plots and characters; his best, however, go beyond the conventions, his own and those of his time, to create genuine art. The *Confessions* impresses because both Robert and Gil-Martin are so strikingly rendered; the *Brownie of Bodsbeck* works because the emotions are so human; the ghost stories convince because the tone is so objective and accepting; and the comedies entertain because they have a joyful sense of humor. This humor, too, knows no bounds—it can penetrate the Bishop of Carlisle's wine-cellar or it can occur in the most serious occasions. During the terrors of Robert's flight in the *Confessions*, for example, he meets a Dickensian Mr. Jingle who has seen the devil in the printshop: "Saw him myself, gave him a nod, and good-day. Rather a gentlemanly personage—Green Circassian hunting coat and turban—Like a foreigner—Has the power of vanishing in one moment though—Rather a suspicious circumstance that. Otherwise, his appearance not much against him" (*Con*, 223). This comic passage, coming when it does, is the "antisyzygy" with a vengeance, but it is the man as well. Because so much of Hogg pervades his works, literally and figuratively, their limitations are those of the man himself: simple, unintellectual, optimistic. But the achievements of the works also reflect the strengths of the man: a gift for song and for conveying the supernatural, a propensity for comedy, for entertainment, and for the enjoyment of life. If he is a minor writer, it is because he does not explore the total range or depth of human experience. But what he was capable of doing—especially in evoking the supernatural world—he did well. The man and his work are so intertwined that it seems fitting to close a discussion of his works with a poem, not one of his best, perhaps, but one most characteristic; he placed it at the end of his collection of *Songs*:

> Oh, we had wander'd far an' wide
>   O'er Scotia's hill, o'er firth an' fell,
> An' mony a simple flower we've cull'd,
>   An' trimm'd them wi' the heather bell!
>
> Though I was wayward, you were kind,
>   And sorrow'd when I went astray;
> For, oh, my strains were often wild
>   As winds upon a winter day.
>
> If e'er I led you from the way,
>   Forgie your Minstrel aince for a';
> A tear fa's wi' his parting lay,—
>   Good night, and joy be wi' you a'!
>                 (*Poems*, 439)

# Notes and References

### Preface

1. Cited in Mrs. [Mary Gray Hogg] Garden, *Memorials of James Hogg, The Ettrick Shepherd* (London: Alexander Gardner, 1887), p. 64.

### Chapter One

1. John Gibson Lockhart, *The Life of Sir Walter Scott, Bart.* (London: Adam and Charles Black, 1893), p. 248.

2. Prof. J. F. Ferrier, quoted in Mrs. Garden, p. 59.

3. Alan L. Strout, "James Hogg's Birthday," *Times Literary Supplement*, 15 February 1936, p. 139.

4. *Works of the Ettrick Shepherd*, ed. Rev. Thomas Thomson (London: Blackie and Son, 1866), II, p. 71n; hereafter Hogg's poetry will be cited textually as *Poems*. Michael Scott took his revenge by making his rival dance herself to death (*Poems*, 25n.).

5. Mrs. Garden, p. 5.

6. *Works*, I, p. 409; hereafter Hogg's prose will be cited textually as *Tales*.

7. Mrs. Garden, p. 5.

8. Ibid., p. 173.

9. Cited by Douglas S. Mack, ed., *James Hogg: Memoir of the Author's Life* and *Familiar Anecdotes of Sir Walter Scott* (Edinburgh: Scottish Academic Press, 1972), p. vii. Hereafter, quotations from this edition will be cited textually as *Mem* or *FA*.

10. *Prize Essays and Transactions of the Highland Society of Scotland*, Second Series 3 (1832): 281-306.

11. Later, Hogg added her charge: "Ye hae broken the charm now, an' they'll never be sung mair" (*FA*, 137).

12. *The Spy*, No. 52 (11 September 1811), p. 411; hereafter cited textually as *Spy*. Fewer than ten complete sets exist (*Mem* 22n).

13. Hogg wrote Scott a letter beginning "Damned Sir" and concluding "Yours, with disgust," and refused to meet with him. However, when Hogg became seriously ill after an extended drinking bout, Scott approached Grieve to make sure that the poet received proper medical

attention. On his recovery, Hogg wrote an abject letter of apology, and they were reconciled. In his last years, Hogg himself refused to contribute to a similar project, even quoting Scott's proverb that it's best "to let every herring hang by its own head" (Mrs. Garden, p. 315).

14. The fullest account of Hogg's part in the "Chaldee MS." occurs in Strout, "James Hogg's 'Chaldee Manuscript,' " *PMLA* 65 (September 1950): 695-718.

15. Lockhart, p. 453.

16. Mrs. Garden, pp. 198-99.

17. Ibid., pp. 254-55.

18. Ibid., pp. 258, 262.

19. Lockhart, p. 760.

20. The tribute is undercut by the headnote describing Hogg as "undoubtedly a man of original genius, but of coarse manners, and low offensive opinions."

## Chapter Two

1. See Douglas Mack's extensive notes and commentary in *Mem* for the significant changes. The "fourth" version refers to the second edition of *Mountain Bard*.

2. In the *Confessions*, for instance, Hogg writes of an "unguent hard to be swallowed" (*The Private Memoirs and Confessions of a Justified Sinner*, ed. John Carey [London: Oxford University Press, 1970], p. 2; hereafter cited as *Con*). Also, see below, p. 65.

3. Lockhart tells of an early visit to Scott in which Hogg's clothes "bore most legible marks of a recent sheep-smearing." He "dined heartily and drank freely, and, by jest, anecdote, and song, afforded plentiful merriment to the more civilized part of the company." As the evening wore on, Hogg treated both Scotts with improper familiarity, though he later apologized (Lockhart, pp. 111-12).

4. Hogg's handling of the publication of *The Queen's Wake*, probably due to inexperience, led to serious and bitter difficulties with George Goldie and Constable; see Edith C. Batho, *The Ettrick Shepherd* (New York: Greenwood Press, 1969), pp. 69-70.

5. Wilson's review of the *Memoir* in *Blackwood's* (10 [August 1821]: 43-52) was so savage that it had to be recast in the form of an anonymous letter *to* Wilson. See Strout, "Authorship of the Review 'On Hogg's Memoirs' in *Blackwood's*, 1821," *Notes and Queries* 181 (29 November 1941): 302-303.

6. Quoted in Henry Thew Stephenson, *The Ettrick Shepherd: A Biography* (Bloomington: Indiana University Press, 1922), p. 99.

7. Only in the disagreements with Blackwood and Wordsworth does Hogg seem uncharacteristically unforgiving. Although reconciled with the

former, Hogg let stand his reaction to a supposed slight by Wordsworth (*Mem*, 70).

8. See Batho; Mrs. Garden; and Strout, *The Life and Letters of James Hogg, The Ettrick Shepherd* (Lubbock: Texas Tech Press, 1946).

9. *Fraser's Magazine* 3 (February 1831): 23-24. Strout, in "The *Noctes Ambrosianae*, and James Hogg" (*Review of English Studies* 13 [January and April 1937]: 46-63, 177-89) gives a picture of the Shepherd of the *Noctes*.

10. *Tales*, p. 422. Hector had become renowned by figuring as the subject of one of Hogg's early poems; see below, pp. 56-57.

11. *A Short Introduction to Scottish Literature* (Edinburgh: Serif Books, 1951), p. 22.

12. *Lay Sermons* (London: Fraser, 1834), p. vi.

13. Ibid., p. v.

14. Quoted in Stephenson, pp. 98-99. See also Hogg's letter to his brother about boarding his nephew: "Proficiency in counting and arithmetic is of ten times more importance for a young man, who has his way to make in the world, than a knowledge of the classics. . . . There is not as much time misspent on anything in this age as the learning of Latin by thousands and thousands of boys to whom it is of no avail" (Mrs. Garden, pp. 49-50).

15. See Strout, "James Hogg's *Familiar Anecdotes of Sir Walter Scott*," *Studies in Philology* 33 (July 1936): 456-74; and Mack, *FA*, ix, xiii-xiv.

16. Lockhart objected not only to Hogg's self-aggrandizement, but also to a suggestion of Lady Scott's illegitimacy and to a description of Scott in his final illness as being like "a man mortally drunk" (*FA*, 131). But Mack points out that the story of Lady Scott was a common rumor and that Hogg certainly meant no slight (*FA*, 110n.). Likewise, the image of Scott was meant to be visually accurate and not disrespectful.

17. *Fraser's Magazine* 10 (August 1834): 125-56.

18. Strout, *Life and Letters*, pp. 226-27.

*Chapter Three*

1. Mrs. Garden, p. 68.

2. *The Three Perils of Man*, ed. Douglas Gifford (Edinburgh: Scottish Academic Press, 1972), p. 302; hereafter cited textually as *3PM*.

3. *Fraser's Magazine* 11 (June 1835): 666-79.

4. "Some Observations of the Poetry of the agricultural and that of the pastoral Districts of Scotland," *Blackwood's Magazine* 4 (February 1819): 527.

5. Ibid.

6. See Kurt Wittig's discussion of "near-English, Anglo-Scots, or Scots-English," in *The Scottish Tradition in Literature* (Edinburgh: Oliver and Boyd, 1958), pp. 201ff.

7. *Fraser's Magazine* 11 (March 1835): 357-59.

8. For example, in *3PM* Hogg tells a superb story of Sandy Yellowlees, a fisherman who discovers how the besieged castle is receiving supplies and then intercepts them for his own use until captured and executed. Likewise, the fine tale of "Marion's Jock" and the poem "When the Kye comes Hame" appear here first.

9. (London: Longmans, 1823), II. 242; hereafter as *3PW*.

### Chapter Four

1. His titles indicate their history: "A Tale of Pentland," "A Story of Good Queen Bess," "A Story of the Forty-Six," *Tales of the Wars of Montrose*. Occasionally, like Scott, Hogg goes abroad: Basil Lee, for instance, fights in the American Revolution, and John Lochy under Marlborough in the Continental wars; but eventually they return to Scotland, where they (and Hogg) seem more comfortable.

2. *Old Mortality*, Chapter 35.

3. "Strange Letter," *Fraser's Magazine* 2 (December 1830): 526-32; "The Pongos," originally "A Singular Letter from Southern Africa," *Blackwood's Magazine* 26 (November 1829): 809-16, later reprinted in *Altrive Tales* (London: James Cochrane, 1832); "Allan Gordon," *Tales and Sketches* (Edinburgh: Blackie and Son, 1837), Vol. I.

### Chapter Five

1. "Hogg's Tales, &c.," *Blackwood's Magazine* 7 (May 1820): 154.

2. *Tales of the Wars of Montrose* (London: James Cochrane, 1835), II, 189-90; subsequent references in text.

3. *Selected Poems of James Hogg* (Oxford: Oxford University Press, 1970), p. xxi.

4. Mrs. Garden, p. 243.

5. "The Bush aboon Traquair; or, The Rural Philosophers," *Tales and Sketches* (1837), II, 298-99; subsequent references in text.

6. "A Screed on Politics," *Blackwood's Magazine* 37 (April 1835): 364.

7. "Chaldee Manuscript," reprinted in John Wilson, *Noctes Ambrosianae*, ed. J. F. Ferrier (Edinburgh: Blackwood, 1864), IV, 291-318. Hogg's original is cited in Strout, *Life and Letters*, p. 134.

8. See Hogg's letter to Blackwood in 1821 complaining about the "ribaldry and mockery . . . vomited forth on me" in his magazine (Strout, *Life and Letters*, p. 224).

9. Quoted in Stephenson, p. 49.

## Chapter Six

1. "A Tale of an Old Highlander," *Metropolitan* 3 (February 1832): 119.

2. Mrs. Garden, p. 50.

3. Cited in Strout, *Life and Letters*, p. 241.

4. *Poems*, 13; see Mack, *Selected Poems*, pp. xxii-xxvi.

5. Hogg adds a footnote here: "A friend of mine from the country [objected] to this stanza, on the ground of its being false and unphilosophical; 'For ye ken, sir,' said he, 'that wherever a man may be, or can possibly be, whether in a bodily or spiritual state, there maun aye be a firmament aboon his head, and something or other below his feet. In short, it is impossible for a being to be anywhere in the boundless universe in which he winna find baith an *up* and a *down*.' I was obliged to give in, but was so much amused with the man's stubborn incredulity, that I introduced it again in the last part" (*Poems*, 129). Ironically, the Space Age has increased the realism of Hogg's poem.

6. *Fraser's Magazine* 3 (March 1831): 174-80.

7. "The Unearthly Witness," *Fraser's Magazine* 2 (September 1830): 171-78; "Julia M'Kenzie," *Tales*, 579-86.

8. "A Story of the Black Art," *Edinburgh Literary Journal* Nos. 111 and 112 (25 December 1830 and 1 January 1831): 396-99, 10-12.

9. *The Club Book* (London: Cochrane and Pickersgill), III, 231-64.

10. "Cousin Mattie," *Tales and Sketches* (1837), 179-90.

11. "Strange Letter," pp. 530-32.

12. "Introduction," *The Private Memoirs and Confessions of a Justified Sinner* (London: Cresset Press, 1947), p. ix.

13. *The English Novel* (New York: Dutton, 1954), p. 142.

14. More detailed discussion of Gil-Martin can be found in L. L. Lee's "The Devil's Figure: James Hogg's *Justified Sinner*," *Studies in Scottish Literature* 3 (April 1966): 230-39. See also Gide; and Coleman O. Parsons, *Witchcraft and Demonology in Scott's Fiction* (Edinburgh: Oliver and Boyd), pp. 293-96.

15. *James Hogg* (Edinburgh: Ramsay Head Press, 1976), p. 158.

16. Gide, p. xi. See also the background material in Louis Simpson, *James Hogg: A Critical Study* (Edinburgh: Oliver and Boyd, 1962).

17. "The Hunt of Eildon," in *The Tales of James Hogg* (London: Hamilton, Adams and Co., 1880), p. 21. The last four words do not appear in the *Works*, which does contain the abridged *Confessions* that removes references to Robert's prayers, unshaken faith, and assurance of justification—thus "the doctrinal and psychological hinges of the work are . . . patiently unscrewed" (Carey, *Con*, xxvii).

## Chapter Seven

1. Happily, this picture is changing—good critical editions of *Confessions, Three Perils of Man, Memoir* and *Familiar Anecdotes,* and *Brownie of Bodsbeck* have all recently appeared.

2. In Strout, *Life and Letters,* p. 130.

3. Charlotte Brontë, *Miscellaneous and Unpublished Writings* (Oxford: Shakespeare Head Press, 1936), I. 1; Lawrence and E. M. Hanson, *The Four Brontës* (London: Oxford University Press, 1950), p. 44. Winifred Gérin sees *Wuthering Heights* as significantly influenced by the *Confessions*—see *Emily Brontë: A Biography* (Oxford: Clarendon Press, 1971), p. 217.

4. Michael Allen, *Poe and the British Magazine Tradition* (New York: Oxford University Press, 1969), passim.

5. Quoted in Strout, *Life and Letters,* p. 114.

6. *James Hogg* (Edinburgh: Oliphant, Anderson and Ferrier, 1899), p. 9; Stephenson, p. 109.

7. *Scottish Literature* (London: Macmillan and Co., 1919), pp. 4-5.

8. See especially the essays on dialect and on Burns in Wittig and in Smith, *Scottish Literature.*

# Selected Bibliography

PRIMARY SOURCES

*The Spy*. Edinburgh: Constable, 1811.

*Dramatic Tales*. 2 vols. Edinburgh: Ballantyne, 1817.

*Winter Evening Tales*. 2 vols. Edinburgh: Oliver and Boyd, 1820. Includes "Highland Adventures" ("Malise's Tour") and "Love Adventures of Mr. George Cochrane."

*The Three Perils of Man; or, War, Women, and Witchcraft*, ed. Douglas Gifford. Edinburgh: Scottish Academic Press, 1972. Critical edition of the novel originally published in 1822.

*The Three Perils of Woman; or, Love, Leasing, and Jealousy*. 3 vols. London: Longmans, 1823.

*The Private Memoirs and Confessions of a Justified Sinner*, ed. John Carey. London: Oxford University Press, 1970. Critical edition of novel originally published in 1824.

*Altrive Tales*. London: Cochrane, 1832. Includes "Adventures of Captain John Lochy" and "The Pongos."

*Memoir of the Author's Life* and *Familiar Anecdotes of Sir Walter Scott*, ed. Douglas S. Mack. Edinburgh: Scottish Academic Press, 1972. Critical edition of the works which originally appeared in 1832 and 1834, respectively.

*Tales of the Wars of Montrose*. 3 vols. London: Cochrane, 1835. Includes "Sir Simon Brodie."

*Tales and Sketches*. 6 vols. Edinburgh: Blackie and Son, 1837. Includes "Allan Gordon" and "Bush aboon Traquair."

*The Works of the Ettrick Shepherd*, ed. Rev. Thomas Thomson. 2 vols. London: Blackie and Son, 1866. Vol. I: *Tales and Sketches*; Vol. II: *Poems and Ballads*.

In addition, more than a hundred tales, poems, and sketches remain uncollected in contemporary magazines and literary annuals; see the bibliography of Hogg's works in Batho, below.

SECONDARY SOURCES

BATHO, EDITH C. *The Ettrick Shepherd*. New York: Greenwood Press,

1969. A compact, gracefully written 1927 critical biography, with an indispensable bibliography of Hogg's works; it over-praises the lyrics and undervalues the fiction, however.

_____. "Notes on the Bibliography of James Hogg," *Transactions of the Bibliographical Society* 16 (December 1935): 309-26. Adds to and corrects the above bibliography.

DOUGLAS, GEORGE B. S. *James Hogg*. Edinburgh: Oliphant, Anderson and Ferrier, 1899. Kindly, moralizing biography which draws uncritically on the *Memoir*; sees Hogg as a regional writer.

GARDEN, MRS. [MARY GRAY HOGG]. *Memorials of James Hogg, the Ettrick Shepherd*. London: Alexander Gardner, 1903 (3rd ed.). Daughter's tribute designed to correct Lockhart and Wilson portraits of her father; major source of letters and contemporary accounts, which, however, have been heavily cut.

GIFFORD, DOUGLAS. *James Hogg*. Edinburgh: Ramsay Head Press, 1976. An important study which concentrates on the fiction, the Edinburgh literary society, and Hogg's constant "dualism."

LEE, L. L. "The Devil's Figure: James Hogg's *Justified Sinner*," *Studies in Scottish Literature* III (April 1966): 230-39. Fine study of "ambiguous evil" and irony in the *Confessions*.

LOCKHART, JOHN GIBSON. *The Life of Sir Walter Scott, Bart*. London: Adam and Charles Black, 1893. Mentions Hogg often, only occasionally unfairly but always noting his inferiority and rural manners.

MACK, DOUGLAS S., ed. *Selected Poems of James Hogg*. Oxford: Oxford University Press, 1970. Includes commentaries on several poems and a good discussion of language and Christianity in "Kilmeny."

OLIVER, JOHN W. "Scottish Poetry in the Earlier Nineteenth Century," in *Scottish Poetry: A Critical Survey*, ed. James Kinsley. London: Cassell and Company, 1955, pp. 230-33. Brief treatment of the folk background of Hogg's songs.

PARSONS, COLEMAN O. *Witchcraft and Demonology in Scott's Fiction*. London: Oliver and Boyd, 1964, pp. 286-97. Catalogues the supernatural stories and poems, then looks at the psychological Devil in *Confessions*.

SAINTSBURY, GEORGE. "Hogg," *Essays in English Literature*. London: Percival and Co., 1890, pp. 33-66. Leisurely introduction to Hogg's best pieces, though the net effect seems more negative than orginally intended.

SIMPSON, LOUIS. *James Hogg: A Critical Study*. Edinburgh: Oliver and Boyd, 1962. Somewhat mechanical treatments of stories and poems, but with an important discussion of the antinomian background of the *Confessions* and a good bibliography of secondary sources.

SMITH, G. GREGORY. *Scottish Literature: Character and Influence*. London: Macmillan, 1919. Still central to Scottish literary history;

develops the "Caledonian Antisyzygy."

SMITH, SYDNEY GOODSIR. *A Short Introduction to Scottish Literature.* Edinburgh: Serif Books, 1951. Excellent monograph surveying the three main periods, with annotated bibliography of principal readings in Scottish literary history.

STEPHENSON, HENRY THEW. *The Ettrick Shepherd: A Biography.* Indiana University Studies No. 54 (Bloomington: Indiana University, September 1922). Undistinguished and often confusing biography, but with extracts from the hard-to-find *Spy* and *Lay Sermons.*

STROUT, ALAN LANG. *The Life and Letters of James Hogg.* Lubbock: Texas Tech Press, 1946. Vol. I (1770-1825). Meticulously researched biography provides crucial source material, specifically dated, but must be used with Mrs. Garden and Batho; the typescript of Vol. II is in the National Library of Scotland. Strout has also written several important biographical articles.

_____. "James Hogg's *Familiar Anecdotes of Sir Walter Scott*," *Studies in Philology* 33 (July 1936): 456-74. The various revisions of the book and Lockhart's role in the affair.

_____. "The *Noctes Ambrosianae*, and James Hogg," *Review of English Studies* 13 (January and April 1937): 46-63, 177-89. Analysis of the character of Wilson's Shepherd.

WITTIG, KURT. *The Scottish Tradition in Literature.* London: Oliver and Boyd, 1958. Readable literary history sets Scottish literature in the European tradition; relates Hogg to older Scottish verse and discusses levels of reality in the *Confessions.*

# Index